AN INTRODUCTION

TO THE STUDY OF

PASTORAL THEOLOGY

HENRY FROWDE, M.A.
PUBLISHER TO THE UNIVERSITY OF OXFORD
LONDON, EDINBURGH, NEW YORK
TORONTO AND MELBOURNE

AN INTRODUCTION
TO THE STUDY OF
PASTORAL THEOLOGY

BY THE

REV. CLEMENT F. ROGERS, M.A.

LECTURER IN PASTORAL THEOLOGY AT KING'S COLLEGE
UNIVERSITY OF LONDON
AUTHOR OF 'BAPTISM AND CHRISTIAN ARCHAEOLOGY'
'CHARITABLE RELIEF,' AND 'PRINCIPLES OF PARISH WORK'

Ἦ οὐ γελοῖον ἐπὶ μὲν ἄλλοις σμικροῦ ἀξίοις πᾶν ποιεῖν
συντεινομένους ὅπως ὅτι ἀκριβέστατα καὶ καθαρώτατα ἕξει,
τῶν δὲ μεγίστων μὴ μεγίστας ἀξιοῦν εἶναι καὶ τὰς ἀκριβείας;

OXFORD
AT THE CLARENDON PRESS
1912

PREFACE

' It is not merely the standard of efficiency that needs to be raised to the level of that of other professions ; the whole conception of Pastoral Theology needs to be lifted up to a higher plane. To elaborate this idea would require the writing of another book.'

So I wrote six years ago in the last chapter of my *Principles of Parish Work* ; and this is the other book. In that I started from practical experience and sought for principles and laws ; in this I have tried to establish those laws by the wider observation of a more matured experience, and so to bring them to an ordered whole. It has involved many voyages through strange seas of thought ; many of its statements have been subjected to the fire of open criticism ; others have been confirmed by what I have seen in visiting some 110 churches to preach for the cause of religious education. I owe much to books ; more, perhaps, to the living voices of friends ; most, I think, to a growing sense of my own short-comings, which has taught me how great is the need of moulding aright the earthen vessels in which we are to hold the treasures of the Church.

The substance of what I have here written formed the matter of my first lectures to the theological students at King's College, where

I have for four years had the privilege of helping them in their preparation for their calling. But it has always seemed to me that one style suits oral teaching, while for literary expression, with its greater opportunities, quite another is required; and that, if any man thinks he has anything to say to others, he owes it to them to spare no pains to say it in the best way he can ; therefore I have worked over and developed the whole in writing till it has become another thing.

I have to thank the editor of the *Church Quarterly Review* for permission to reprint an article on English and Foreign Schools of Pastoral Theology, which forms a large part of one of the chapters that follow ; the editors of the *Economic Review* and of the *School Guardian*, in which the chapters dealing with Sociology and Education first appeared, and the editors of the *Churchman* and of the *Commonwealth* for allowing me to incorporate short articles from the pages of their magazines. While I am alone responsible for what is here written, my sincerest thanks are due to the Rev. H. B. Jones, Mr. A. W. Jose, the Rev. C. Jenkins, and Prof. J. P. Whitney for words of encouragement, criticism, and advice, which are among the most valuable gifts that friend can give to friend.

CLEMENT F. ROGERS.

1 Vernon Chambers, Southampton Row,
    London, W.C.
      May 1912.

CONTENTS

BOOK I

THE SCIENCE OF PASTORAL THEOLOGY

CHAPTER I

THE NEED OF A SCIENCE

CHAPTER II

THE NATURE OF THE SCIENCE

CHAPTER III

THE LITERATURE OF PASTORAL THEOLOGY

BOOK II

THE AGENT IN PASTORAL THEOLOGY

CHAPTER I

THE WORK OF A CLERGYMAN

CHAPTER II

THE TRAINING OF THE STUDENT

CHAPTER III

THE TRANSITION TO ACTIVE LIFE

BOOK III

THE SCOPE OF PASTORAL THEOLOGY

CHAPTER I

PASTORAL THEOLOGY AND PSYCHOLOGY

CHAPTER II

PASTORAL THEOLOGY AND EDUCATION

CHAPTER III

PASTORAL THEOLOGY AND SOCIOLOGY

CHAPTER IV

THE MATERIAL OF PASTORAL THEOLOGY

BOOK IV

THE METHOD OF PASTORAL THEOLOGY

CHAPTER I

THE FACULTY OF OBSERVATION

CONTENTS

CHAPTER II

THE WORK OF CRITICISM

CHAPTER III

SELECTION AND CLASSIFICATION

CHAPTER IV

GENERALIZATION AND CONSTRUCTIVE WORK

CHAPTER V

THE MACHINERY OF PASTORAL THEOLOGY

BOOK I

THE SCIENCE OF PASTORAL THEOLOGY

' If all parts of knowledge have been thought by wise men to be then most orderly delivered and proceeded in, when they are drawn to their first original ; seeing that our whole question concerneth the quality of ecclesiastical laws, let it not seem a labour superfluous that in the entrance thereunto all these several kinds of laws have been considered, inasmuch as they all concur as principles, they all have their forcible operations therein, though not all in like apparent and manifest manner. By means whereof it cometh to pass that the force which they have is not observed of many.'—HOOKER, *Ecclesiastical Polity*, Book I, xvi. 1.

CHAPTER I

THE NEED OF A SCIENCE

THERE is no need to emphasize the importance of Pastoral Theology ; in its width of range, in the seriousness of its subject-matter, and in the actuality of its problems it stands unrivalled. Where the business man works within the limits of his office, and in the ramifications of one trade, the clergyman works at least on the scale of the parish, with its crossing and complicated interests reaching out to the diocese and stretching over the kingdom. Where the doctor is charged with

The importance of Pastoral Theology.

responsibility for the care of men's bodies, the priest is burdened with that of the cure of souls. The schoolmaster has to be prepared to find that much in education must be mere drudgery, while the parson can confine his actual teaching to the one subject of unfailing interest in the syllabus. The actor presents an illusion theatrically to an audience, but the minister of the sacraments enacts the drama of public worship, with a congregation that not only witnesses, but takes part in, a reality. Where the student of books deals with theory, the pastor deals also with men ; where the journalist traffics in words, his commerce is also with what they signify ; where the orator speaks, he preaches ; where the social worker deals with cases of distress, and seeks for remedies, he is building up in the people the character that forestalls want. The field of other callings is departmental ; his extends to the whole man. To the parson nothing personal or human is foreign. ' Ars est artium regimen animarum.' [1]

[1] Greg. Magn. *De Cura Pastorali*, i. 1.   An oft-quoted saying based on the words of Gregory Nazianzen τῷ ὄντι γὰρ αὕτη μοι φαίνεται τέχνη τις εἶναι τεχνῶν, καὶ ἐπιστήμη ἐπιστημῶν, ἄνθρωπον ἄγειν τὸ πολυτροπώτατον ζῷον καὶ ποικιλώτατον. Oratio II. Apologetica, 16 ; Migne, *P. G.* xxxv, p. 425.   (' For the guiding of men, the most variable and manifold of creatures, seems to me in very deed to be the art of arts and the science of sciences.'   Select Library of Nicene and Post-Nicene Fathers of the Christian Church, ed. H. Wace, D.D., and P. Schaff, D.D., LL.D.   Parker, Oxford, 1894, vol. vii, p. 208.)

I

But the claim made by Chremes in an epigram involves consequences that are not so lightly met.[1] The cure of souls is a difficult task, and when we look round us we realize that neither the agents in Pastoral Theology, nor its various departments of work as now carried out, come as near to this ideal as we should desire. It is true that the criticisms of the anonymous reviewer, and of the irresponsible writer of reminiscences may not count for much, that we need not take too seriously the novelist who wishes to make her books sell, or the playwright whose aim is to amuse his audience. The public they appeal to is, no doubt, prejudiced and ignorant. But a student should not begin by being an apologist ; he should judge himself by a stricter standard than that of popular opinion, and the fact remains that men of other professions, though not claiming to be perfect in their several arts, speak with a quiet authority on their own subjects, and are deferred to with respect as qualified to do so. Their position on their own ground is recognized and their work

Its present condition unsatisfactory.

(a) As regards the agents ;

---

[1] Cicero, *De Officiis* i. 9, 30 : ' Est enim difficilis cura rerum alienarum.   Quanquam Terentianus ille Chremes " humani nihil a se alienum putat "—aliter de illis et de nobis iudicamus.' (It is a hard matter to take active concern in the affairs of others. Although Chremes in the play of Terence thinks nothing human foreign to himself—we judge differently of them and of ourselves.)

is definite. Its sphere is understood by the world—
every one, for instance, knows what a doctor has
to do—and, in the vast majority of cases, it is
carried out competently and efficiently.

It is true also that the task is easier in the case
of the lower callings of life. Since they deal with
concrete and easily intelligible things, we are
always inclined to exaggerate their importance
and to over-estimate the value of what we call
' practical men '. ' Every man,' said Dr. Johnson,
' thinks meanly of himself for not having been
a soldier.' [1] Merchants exert a strange fascination
on those who have responsibilities in the deeper
matters that can only be dealt with by abstractions. When they look at the straightforwardness
and supposed peculiar manliness of the work of
business and military men, they are filled with an
indefinite sense of envy and longing, though all
the time they know that their judgement is being
perverted, and that the real prerogative of man
is just the power to realize the value of things
intellectual and spiritual.

But this is not the sole cause why many, and
those by no means the worst, are turning away
from Holy Orders to choose other careers of public
service. Nor can the decline in number and status
of those who are candidates for Ordination be due
to the fact that a higher standard is now demanded

---

[1] Boswell's *Life*, April 10, 1778.

than was the case in years gone by ; [1] for by
raising the standard of any work, better men are
drawn to it, and it is doubtful if even the number
of those by whom it is sought is diminished.
Moreover, many of the best of our clergy are far
from being satisfied ; they are conscious that,
while in their professional activities they do
nothing that is inconsistent with their normal
and private lives, still, by the tradition and
accepted methods of work that have to be carried
on, they are compelled to be active on different
planes, and to live by unequal standards, in the
one sphere and in the other. They fight against
the secret feeling of envy for the greater practical
efficiency of laymen ; they imagine they are at
a disadvantage in their presence, and have to resist
a continual temptation to be over-anxious to defer
to their opinion, or else to assert themselves
unduly in order to maintain their self-confidence.
Or, sometimes, they plunge into what is really
secular and lay work ; they visit, they run
boys' clubs, they serve as Guardians, &c., because
here they feel is something clear, ordered,
straightforward, and definite.

When we turn from the agents in Pastoral (b) As
Theology to the work itself, the same thing meets regards
us. Again, the casual remarks of laymen who work.
stand outside and criticize are of little value,

[1] Last year the numbers went up a little. It is to be hoped
that they will continue to rise.

B 2

but many that are made ought not to be possible
even as exaggerations.   It is not enough to point
out that anticlerical prejudice has an extraordinary power of distorting the judgement of
men, otherwise moderate and reasonable, for it
may be argued on the other side with equal
truth, that popular judgement is often too lenient,
since unprejudiced outsiders always tend to over-
estimate the efficiency and thoroughness of work
that they know little or nothing about.   Still,
it would not be resented as unfair to say that in
matters pastoral we have an unsatisfactory standard.   For teaching in Sunday schools, for parish
work, for choirs, we are too often content with
amateur, untrained effort ;   in mere business
arrangements, in finance, in correspondence, we
do not insist on the conditions that are demanded
elsewhere ;   our methods are far too traditional
and have in many points become out of date ; we
need far more power of grasping new situations,
and of adapting our undertakings to changed
conditions.   And the seriousness of it all lies
in the fact that, though we have developed and
increased our work in many ways, the type
has remained the same, and the standard is
practically unchanged, while both type and
standard in all other professions and callings have
advanced.[1]

[1] Cp. my *Circumstances or Character?* (Methuen, 1911)
p. 58 : ' The Origins of modern " Church Work ".'

What has been the cause of advance in other callings ? For to discover this will help us, it may be, to see the way to progress in Pastoral Work. There can be little doubt that the advance of the last generation, which has not been an age of great men, has been mainly due to the influence of science, and to the application of scientific method to all departments of human knowledge and action.

The influence of science has been general, but it has been most prominent in Physics and Biology. Its practical use in applied mechanical arts, in Agriculture and Medicine, has been bewildering. So prominent has this development been that Natural Science from the mere fact of conspicuousness has come to usurp the name of Science itself, and, by a vulgar error similar to that which leads men to speak of Roman Catholics s ' Catholics ', the term ' Science ' is commonly ed, even by scientific theologians, to denote lowest in the whole hierarchy of sciences.

he corresponding development in the higher more human sciences has, however, been ss remarkable. Art criticism has ceased name pictures by guesswork, and notes the idiosyncrasies of each master. Dates are not now assigned to antiquities haphazard, but by fixed canons of criticism. Archaeology, from being a me ollecting of antiquities, has become an exac e which has revolutionized our ideas about Greek religion, and has unveiled the history of ancient and forgotten civilizations ; so that museums are no longer mere curiosity shows, but places for serious work.

In directly human studies which deal with the bodily and intellectual life of man, the same change has been brought about. Anthropology has taken the place of travellers' tales. Sociology and organized charity have arisen out of empirical almsgiving. The science of Economics is recognized as the basis of good government, that of Psychology as a necessary preliminary to the work of education. Wild men of the woods are, it is true, still shown at fairs, there is still much promiscuous dole-giving, votes are entrusted to ignorant men, and ' Christian Science ' flourishes, but it is with scientific study and efficient practice in these various departments of human life that future advance lies.

Nor has Theology been left behind. Dealing as it does with the highest faculties of man, it has become no less scientific. The eighteenth-century theories of the pure Theism of the noble savage have disappeared before the comparative study of religions ; the Bible has been given back to us by the very process of criticism that men feared would destroy its authority ; a revival in the study of the history of Dogma has given us a clearer understanding of our inheritance of Christian thought from the past.

But pastoral work remains almost untouched by this spirit. The results of the scientific study of Theology at the Universities remain unpopularized. The gross ignorance of the ordinary layman on matters theological is surprising. The marked difference between the knowledge of students of Divinity and, say, the typical member of Parliament or country squire, who, as a rule, gets his ideas on such subjects as they come to him diluted by the popular magazines and newspapers, witnesses to the almost complete failure of official teaching from the pulpits. The methods of work are for the most part merely traditional ; the estimate of their value, whether right or wrong, rests only on opinion. As a consequence, the divergence between the character of lay and clerical work is growing, and it is to be feared that there is a corresponding continual divergence between the mentality of laymen and of the clergy. *Pastoral Theology untouched.*

The reasons are, surely, the same both in the case of men and of work. Men are largely made what they become by the nature of their duties ; the advance on the one side has been effected by the application of scientific method ; what is wanted on the other is a scientific treatment of Pastoral Theology. *Need of a science of Pastoral Theology.*

II

The meaning of scientific treatment.

Now, what do we mean by scientific treatment ? And, if it be granted that it is by its adoption that the change has been wrought in other branches of knowledge and in other professions, is the parallel with Pastoral Theology and with the calling of a clergyman a fair one ? Can scientific method, which is applicable to inanimate and animate nature, and to human life and thought even in its highest conceptions about God, be also applied to Christian life ?   Can there be a science of Pastoral Theology ? These questions have first to be answered.

When we ask what we mean by scientific method, we naturally turn for an answer to the natural sciences, not because they are more important or exhibit the most delicate operations, but because they are simpler, and because modern methods were first elaborated in them. The great change from deduction to induction as the ordinary method of science, begun by Bacon and established by Darwin, has been the cause of the great advance ; and it is chiefly these methods that we have in our minds when we use the word ' scientific '. They may briefly be said to consist, first in observation and experiment, as, for instance, when the water of solutions is allowed to evaporate in order to find out and to register the shapes of crystals, and then in the collection of data and in generalization of laws, as, for example, in classifying the processes of entomology.

But can this be done in Pastoral Theology? In dealing with spiritual life observation is difficult and precarious, and experiment impossible or, at least, dangerous. You do not see characters crystallizing, nor can you try, like the daughters of Pelias, to re-shape human life in a cauldron. ' How can things immaterial be classified ? ' it may be asked. ' You cannot collect feelings like butterflies.' ' The things of the spirit,' it is argued, ' like the wind, are subject to no laws.' [1] So the possibility of a science of Pastoral Theology is denied, and the denial is based on the practical difficulties which stand in the way, or on the assumption that spiritual things are of so essentially different a nature from material that their phenomena cannot be reduced to laws.

When, however, we come to examine these two objections, what do they amount to ? Without in the least underrating the difficulties in the way, we may urge that the first comes to little more than saying that so far they have not been overcome, and that the second either arises from mere confusion of thought in associating science exclusively with natural studies, or is a confession of mental feebleness which declares human reason

Can there be a Science of Pastoral Theology?

---

[1] I need not point out the equivocation involved in the use of the term ' law ', nor the error in Meteorology made in the statement.

incapable of doing in the highest spheres what it is doing in all the others. If it be argued that the things of God cannot be comprehended by the human mind, the statement is a mere truism ; if it is meant that the things which can be understood about God's dealing with men cannot be reduced to a science, that is to declare that they are irrational.

III

The meaning of science.
What, then, is the meaning of science ? What is the essence of this method that has so changed our view of the world ? Science is ordered knowledge, and is based on a whole-hearted confidence in our mental powers, on a belief that the world is rational, a kosmos and not a chaos, that it ' means intensely and means good ', and that its meaning can be found out and understood by reason. The limitations of reason do not prevent its having full power in its own dominion. Feeling and will may go beyond it, but nothing intelligible may be arbitrarily withdrawn from its scrutiny. These mental powers may be turned on themselves for knowledge about themselves, testing and examining and criticizing their movements, and so creating abstract or normative sciences, such as Metaphysics, Philosophy, Historics, Aesthetics, Ethics, or Logic, or they may be turned on external phenomena to penetrate to their real nature, to

classify them and to generalize from their attributes
and motions—the method adopted for positive
or applied sciences such as Rhetoric, Medicine,
Teaching, or Architecture.

So science was the great gift that Greece gave
to the world. Socrates by his dialectic aimed at
turning opinion into knowledge ; Plato represents
him testing the meaning of words, examining into
the validity of arguments, seeking for truth above
all things. Aristotle set himself to correlate all
knowledge and to bring all things to the bar of
reason. The world is still divided into those who
have submitted to the influence of Greece and
those who have not.

What are the ways in which a man acts in Four
coming to knowledge ? They may conveniently stages in scien-
be grouped under four heads, namely, definition, tific
observation, criticism, and synthesis. These method:
alone can provide a sure foundation on which
constructive work can be based.

The first requisite for advance in any depart- (a) defi-
ment of knowledge is concentration. You must nition,
fix your attention on the subject in hand, and
mentally separate it from all others. Thus so
long as the study of Astronomy was confused with
that of Astrology it made no great advance. As
soon as it was emancipated and studied by itself—
though in relation to Physics generally—the era
of discovery began. But people are quite vague
as to what Pastoral Theology is. The first step,

therefore, is to define the subject, and to consider its relation to Theology generally.[1]

(b) observation, Then must follow observation. The change of mental attitude involved in the Baconian proverb, ' Nature is conquered by being obeyed,' consists in looking to see what really does happen before framing theories instead of merely searching for illustrations of theories already made. It was this change of method that transmuted Alchemy, with its fruitless search for the Elixir of Life and the Philosopher's Stone, into Chemistry that has done so much to combat disease and death and has so enormously enriched the world. The whole method of modern science, with its accurate vision, its careful note-taking, and its training of the eye, is based on the recognition of this need of observation. This humble attitude of the learner, in the face of facts, is the second necessity for scientific method ; the temper of the agent in Pastoral Theology must be that of the student rather than that of the teacher ; we, too, need systematic records, and all the preliminary mechanism of a science, and, what is far more important, the observing faculty to note the phenomena of spiritual life.[2]

(c) criticism, Criticism follows the collection of illustrations. Much that is noticed is irrelevant, much deceptive. The value of every document must be tested, the

---

[1] See below, Book I, ch. ii, and Book III.
[2] See below, Book IV, ch. i.

validity of every illustration tried. To take an example from one of the higher sciences, which are more delicate as dealing with human minds : In old days Archaeology was the mere collecting of curiosities ; at most questions were asked as to their ' genuineness '. Nowadays it is recognized that the value of an article depends on its provenance, the place and the precise layer of finds from which it came ; if this is known, any object discovered may prove to be of great importance. In Pastoral Theology, therefore, we need to be on our guard against blindness to the significance of little things on the one hand, and, on the other hand, to be cautious in accepting statements of popular religious literature. We must rigidly test the assumptions on which schemes are to be built, insist on accuracy of statement, even in advertisements and begging appeals, and criticize every ideal that has been accepted long enough to have become conventional or disregarded.[1]

Synthesis must follow the testing of the data which have been collected. Otherwise they remain a mass of confused evidence. So Medical Science studies sickness by putting together all that it observes. Patients are collected in hospitals ; each case is carefully watched. An institution or a doctor will specialize on one disease ; its complications with others will be noticed. Specialists will then confer ; experience

(d) synthesis and construction.

[1] See below, Book IV, ch. ii.

will be exchanged in the medical papers, and so
gradually a mass of well-tested knowledge is accu-
mulated to which opposition is only made by
quacks and cranks.[1]   Mr. C. Booth's work on *The
Religious Influences of London* represents a similar
undertaking in the area of Pastoral Theology, but
it stands almost alone, and it cannot be said that
the mass of information it contains has been
adequately considered and corroborated, or corrected by other similar investigations.   Until this
has been done, it is impossible to feel that we have
arrived at sound judgements on many important
points.[2]

For constructive action can only follow after
a synthesis of tested data.   Only so can it be
sure and effective.   In one of the highest sciences,
one both pure and applied, namely that of politics,
it was the scientific study of Economics in the
eighteenth century that preceded the great practical reforms of the nineteenth.   England gained
her commercial supremacy because she was bold
enough to trust herself to the conclusions at which
her master-minds had arrived.   But can it be

[1] C. Booth, *Life and Labour of the People of London,* third
series (Macmillan, 1902).   An excellent and thorough investigation of the life and work of the various German State
Churches is in course of production under the title *Evan-
gelische Kirchenkunde,* edited by Professor Paul Drews (Mohr,
Tübingen).

[2] The anti-vaccination and anti-vivisection agitations do
not at all affect the progress of medical science.

said that, except in cases of individuals to individuals, people look to the Church for a lead in any
of the great moral questions of the day, such as
that of divorce, of drink, of the responsibilities
of wealth, or is it from the stage, from novels,
from the daily press, that they get what confused ideas they have to guide their lives and
actions ?

What is the cause of the progress of these Pro-
sciences and of the success of the callings that gress
rest on them ?   It is that their students have scientific
acted on the belief that their methods would be method.
rewarded, and the results have justified their faith.
The leaders in Physical Science have at least been
Monists, and their belief in the universal reign of
law has led them to success.   The pioneers in the
higher sciences have acted on the assumption
that man and his perceptions of the world are
rational, and, just because his rationality has been
unquestioned, their success has been still more
striking.   Theology has always been based on faith
in God as the Eternal Reason, and has succeeded
through all the ages, in all departments of life, and
for all men, in being the inspiration and guide
of wisdom.   And Pastoral Theology will be rewarded in the same way if it adopts the same
methods.

So when the judicious Hooker was confronted
with the great practical problem of his day, his
first step was to make a preliminary consideration

of his mental postulates.[1]   He began, as a true man of science, by considering the nature of Law, of the First Law Eternal, of the Law of Nature, of the Law of Angels or Moral Law, of positive Human Law, of the supernatural and Ecclesiastical Law of Revelation.   To this he devoted the first four books of his *Ecclesiastical Polity*, before he took up the points of his adversaries one by one in the fifth.   As a consequence what might have been an occasional pamphlet of controversy became one of the world's classics.   ' For,' as he asked, ' is there anything which can either be thoroughly understood, or soundly judged of, till the very first causes and principles from which originally it springeth be made manifest ? ' [2]

[1] Cp. R. C. Moberly, *Ministerial Priesthood* (Murray, second edition, 1907), Preface to the first edition, p. xl.

[2] *Ecclesiastical Polity*, Book I. xvi. 1.

CHAPTER II

THE NATURE OF THE SCIENCE OF PASTORAL THEOLOGY

SCIENTIFIC progress appears in two forms ; on the one side there is the actual advance of each science in itself, and on the other the development of the various practical uses to which it is put. In most departments of knowledge there are pure and applied sciences. As a rule, owing to the priority in history of the deductive method, the pure or abstract studies were first built up ; since the time of Bacon the tendency has been to pay more attention to the applied. Thus the laws of mathematics were worked out, before they were generally applied to Astronomy, and long before they were made use of in engineering. The duties of conduct occupied men's attention from the first, no doubt, but the abstract consideration of ethics preceded systematic moral education by many years. In other cases the pairs of subjects have been elaborated almost side by side ; Medicine has had little more than a logical precedence of Therapeutics, while the main interest in the study of Economics has been the immediate value of its political and commercial applications.

The difference between pure and applied, or between abstract and practical, is naturally more

Pure and applied sciences.

The parallel of Social Work.

marked in the more human sciences. Thus in recent years almsgiving has in many places become scientific. The aim of organization in charity has been to enlist the higher services of the mind in order to make it efficient, to discover the laws by which its power to heal works best, and to attain, as near as may be, certainty of results. From the large area of practical observation open to Charity Organization Societies their workers are able, after many years' service, to deduce conclusions about social sickness with the same confidence as that with which doctors pronounce about bodily disease. But the need of broader sociological knowledge is felt by all thoughtful men engaged in such work who set themselves to consider the many questions that lie behind their practical experience. They study the history and nature of the family, the various tendencies of races, the influence of external conditions, the force of heredity, the effect of occupation on character, and so build up their whole theory of the social relationships of man to man.

A similar problem lies before us in Pastoral Theology. We may begin in our parishes, and by hard disciplined thought try to make our work effective, searching out by what spiritual laws the healing of souls may be furthered, so that we may fight the powers of evil in heavenly places not as those that beat the air. With so many workers in the field we could in time earn the right to speak from our experience as to what helps or hinders the growth of spiritual life, with the same confidence that teachers have in speaking of what aids the development of the child-mind. But we also need students of theory who will set themselves to consider on what all our practical work is based, men who will take a wider view, who will compare the religious customs of different countries, who will test the present by the past, who will study the variations and the unchanging features of religious life, who will collect and order all that there is to be known, and build up a body of sound knowledge. But the two must be worked out side by side ; if empirical action is dangerous, to theorize without regard to facts is no less useless.

I

In setting about the creation of these pairs of sciences, the natural process is first to consider the exact nature of the subject to be studied, and then to search for the best methods by which to gain an accurate knowledge of its features.

The exact nature of the subject must first be determined so that attention may be concentrated on it. Otherwise, we shall be like casual visitors to a museum, who wander aimlessly through its galleries ; our efforts will go off into mere desultory reading, conversation, or thought. More particu-

What is Pastoral Theo- logy ?

larly under the conditions of modern life do we feel the need of specialization, but, even in days when the sum of things known was less, wise men distrusted versatility,[1] and popular sentiment has ever since distrusted Jacks-of-all-trades. We have to take our subject and ' scour it clean ', as Glaucon did the characters of the just and of the unjust man,[2] viewing it as a whole and in its subdivisions, and setting it in antithesis or relation to those that are akin but distinct.

What, then, is Pastoral Theology, and what is its relation to Theology as a whole ?

Theology may be defined as the Science of God, and since by a science we mean an ordered department of human knowledge, Theology may be said to deal with the relationships of man to God as presented to the reason.

Theology and Pastoral Theology.   Of this science Pastoral Theology is a part. As a social being man has certain relationships to his fellow man, and some of these meet his or his fellow man's relationships to God.   Pastoral Theology deals with these as they co-operate or clash ; its subject-matter is, therefore, man's share in the relationships of his fellow man to God.   It deals with all that man can do to minister to, or help, the communion of man with God.   Even if it were argued that each man stood absolutely alone, and the possibility of human mediation were

---

[1] Plato, *Republic*, Book III, 398 A.
[2] Ib., Book II, 361 D.

denied, a science would be needed to prove this absolute individualism.[1]

If these are correct definitions of Theology and Pastoral Theology, it will be seen that the two are related but are to be distinguished.   Every theological question has its pastoral side, but to confuse the two while studying them is as fatal as to ignore the one or the other.   When once they are differentiated, their bearing on one another is realized and the value of each is seen.

Thus, Old Testament study is quite different from Old Testament teaching.   Theology studies the origin of the books of which the Hebrew Bible is composed, the exact meaning of the words of the Prophets, the development of the Jewish Law, the evolution of the idea of sacrifice, the growth of moral ideas, the relationship of Israelitish customs to those of surrounding tribes, the genius of Hebrew poetry, the purification of the

In Old Testament Study.

---

[1] Practical Theology, on the other hand, is applied Theology. The term is often used as equivalent to Pastoral Theology, and has been the accepted term in Germany since the time of Schleiermacher, but though its subject-matter is almost coterminous with that of Pastoral Theology, its conception is somewhat different.   It emphasizes the results rather than the agent.   It is more closely allied to Politics, while Pastoral Theology has greater affinity with Psychology.   It is the term expressing the attitude more naturally adopted among those Protestant bodies which have little conception of corporate life or of the need of an organized ministry, while Pastoral Theology is preferred by Catholic Christians who have a constant sense of their relationship to one another and to the Orders of their Church.

conception of God as He gradually revealed Himself to the Chosen People. Pastoral Theology, on the other hand, has quite other tasks. It is concerned with the value of the Old Testament, the distinguishing of the transitory and local from the permanent and universal in its teachings, its practical use in education, the problem of recasting our traditional lessons without losing what is essential, the use of its chapters or psalms in public worship.

Dogmatics.   Again, the study of dogma and of the history of dogma is quite different from Homiletics. The one is part of Theology, the other the counterpart of Pastoral Theology. Theology studies the attempts of man to explain the things of God at the bar of reason ; Pastoral Theology is concerned to show why doctrine matters. When the theological student has examined the reasons for man's belief in God, the student of Pastoral Theology considers how he may so dress them that they may become effective in Apologetics. Where the one studies the Christological controversies of the fourth and fifth centuries, the other ponders on their bearing on modern life, and in their light sees how

> The acknowledgement of God in Christ,
> Accepted by the reason, solves for thee
> All questions in the earth and out of it,
> And hath so far advanced thee to be wise.[1]

In the study of Dogmatics, to preach is fatal;

[1] R. Browning, *A Death in the Desert.*

it is the avowed aim of Homiletics. As a student of Theology, a man examines the meaning and growth of creeds ; when he turns to Pastoral Theology he considers their use in public worship. He first studies for truth's sake, clearing from his mind all thought of edification ; then he takes what he has studied without bias, and ' pastoralizes ' it by recasting it into a useful lesson to be taught to others.

It is, perhaps, in the realm of history that it is History. most necessary to mark the contrast. So long as history was written for a political purpose, to establish or refute a religious creed, or to serve as edifying literature, it was not, properly speaking, history. It is essential for historical honesty that the facts of the past should be approached without being coloured by preconceived ideas. But the mere study of the past is a singularly uninteresting and purposeless occupation, unless afterwards the results are to be used for guidance in the present, to vindicate the truth, or to cultivate the intelligence and character of men. So, to study ecclesiastical history in order to prove a doctrine, or to justify the claims of a Church, is precisely not the way to study it as a part of Theology ; but when it has been studied honestly and critically, then the whole ground should be gone over again as part of Pastoral Theology, to discover in the past analogies to the things of to-day, to profit by the experience of men who, under other conditions, are found to have been extremely like ourselves, from the succession of events to deduce general laws which will interpret present phenomena, to seek for facts which will illustrate truths, or for examples which will encourage men.

Liturgi-ology.

Or, let us take an example where the temptation is rather to study only the pastoral aspect of the subject. Numbers of little books are written about the conduct of service in church ; verbal discussion of points of ritual assumes still larger proportions in religious circles. The danger ' of falling into some improprieties in the daily service by reading to an audience that requires no exactness ', or the deficiencies of those old-fashioned men who, ' to judge by their per-formance, must have thought reading was reading and preaching was preaching ', have long been subjects of discussion in society.[1] Instruction in the rendering of the liturgy appears in the earliest post-Reformation English treatises on the clergyman's duty.[2] Practical suggestions for the management of the voice and handbooks of Church music have not been wanting. But men have been less ready to realize that behind all this,

[1] Cp. Dr. Johnson's letter to a young clergyman, August 30, 1780, in Boswell's *Life* ; and Jane Austen, *Mansfield Park*, ch. xxxiv.

[2] Cp. George Herbert, *The Country Parson*, ch. vi. ; Gilbert Burnet, *Of the Pastoral Care*, ch. viii. ; Sheridan, *Lectures on the Art of Reading*, criticized by Archbishop Whately in his *Elements of Rhetoric*, Part IV, ch. ii, § 2.

hich is the concern of Pastoral Theology, lies the whole field of liturgical science. The result is that the mass of this literature is superficial and empirical, because it lacks broad principles to guide it. The study of Liturgiology, apart from the needs of one particular Church, reveals certain laws of devotion and worship which must be examined before these details can be elaborated with profit. It is bound up with questions of religious psychology, both of man as an individual and of the crowd. Liturgical study is necessary, if we are to gain an aesthetic sense of what is fit in architecture, in music, in the structure of religious offices, in ceremonial, in the language of prayer both private and public. All this is part of general Theology.

Once more, the study of conduct has been recog- Ethics. nized as a science since the days of Aristotle. The Early Church found herself, from the beginning, face to face with moral problems, which she met as best she could. Theologians have, in later days, set themselves to examine and explain the basis of Christian ethics, while preachers drew up lists of theological and cardinal virtues, or used the Ten Commandments to test the consciences of their flock. In the Roman Church, the whole applied science of moral philosophy has been carefully elaborated from the Pastoral work of the Confessional. But in English Theology, Ethics and casuistry have not been sufficiently brought

together.   The theological and pastoral aspects o.
moral science have not been confused as in the
case of history, nor has one been allowed to obscure
the other, as in that of Dogmatics or Liturgiology,
but the help one might have afforded the other
has not been realized.   There is not even a term
for the Pastoral science ; casuistry has a special
meaning, and is discredited ; moral education is
a popular synonym for secular, or anti-Christian,
schooling ;[1] we have to content ourselves with
the vague term ' Church work ', and the methods
and aims of this ' Church work ' cannot be said to
have been studied scientifically.

II

The creation of the student.
Our next task is to find out the best method of
gaining an accurate knowledge of the features
of Pastoral Theology.   For this our prime need is
to create the right type of student.   We require
a class of specialists who possess the peculiar
faculty of concentration, who can fix their attention on their particular study and notice just that
which bears on it.

This has been secured in other callings.   The
artist trains his sense of colour and of form.
The schoolmaster acquires the ' teacher's eye '.

[1] For an example, however, of a work in which the term
is used in its exact meaning see *Moral Instruction and Training
in Schools*.   Report of an International Inquiry, edited by
M. E. Sadler (Longmans, 1908).

he botanist detects varieties where others see only yellow primroses. The cobbler notes more than Apelles when he looks at a sandal. To the man in the street a boy crying papers suggests merely a convenient way of getting the news ; the social worker is conscious of the whole terrible problem of the ruin of child-life by street-selling. So far did Darwin carry this special faculty of concentration that he complained in latter life that he had become a machine for grinding out facts.

So we require students who have acquired this initial qualification for building up a science of Pastoral Theology. On a basis of a sound knowledge of general Theology they must learn to specialize. They must learn to be sensitive to spiritual issues and sure in their judgements of the values of religious life. They must become able to pick out all that concerns man's work in helping his fellow man in his relationships with God. They must study and sift all that is written on the matter. They must have that belief in working with the head and in the value of ideas which makes the man of science. *Of theory*

For the applied science it is the institutions and objective phenomena that are to be noted rather than abstract ideas. This is largely a matter of classification and method. Many excellent and penetrating sociologists cannot deal with people in distress, and the work of the academic student of Pastoral Theology needs to be translated into *and practice.*

action by practical men. Such students will build
up the machinery of organization and learn by
experiment with things themselves. They have to
get experience, to acquire confidence and tact.
Their method is generally inductive, their besetting
danger empiricism, but their work is no less
scientific than that of the student of ideas.

In other words, we are here confronted with the
old question of the relative values of thought and
dexterity. The former needs to be emphasized as
the basis of the latter, and all the more because
practical work is always more vivid and attractive.
The rival claims of the two may be seen bidding
for the adhesion of man through the whole course
of history wherever we find the contrast of the
active and contemplative life, whether figured in
the images of Leah and Rachel,[1] of Matilda and

---

[1] Greg. Magn. *Epist.* IV, lib. 1 : ' Contemplativae vitae
pulchritudinem velut Rachelem dilexi sterilem sed videntem
et pulchram, quae etsi per quietem suam minus generat,
lucem tamen subtilius videt. Lea mihi in nocte coniuncta est,
activa videlicet vita fecunda sed lippa, minus videns quamvis
amplius parens.'

(' I have loved the beauty of the life of contemplation,
like Rachel barren, but clear-sighted and fair, which, if it by
its quiet bears less fruit, sees the light more subtly. But Leah
has been brought to me in the night, the life of action, fruitful
but tender-eyed, seeing less though bringing more to birth.')

Dante, *Purg.* xxvii. 108 :

Lei lo vedere, e me l' ovrare appaga.

(Her joy
In contemplation, as in labour mine.)

Beatrice,[1] or of Martha and Mary; but we have good authority for asserting that Mary's is the better part—perhaps just because she, by thinking first about her work, got through her share the sooner, and so was at leisure to sit at her Master's feet and learn.

III

Pastoral Theology makes a great claim on the student. For, since it is a practical science, to be a student in it means ultimately to be a priest. To remain in an attitude of detachment permanently is impossible.

The claim on the student.

It is true, of course, of all sciences that there is no progress made in them without application. No one goes forward in any knowledge without paying the price and giving up a great deal, at any rate, in externals. The quest of the Grail inevitably broke up King Arthur's Court. Further, for the understanding of any lore the fit temper is necessary; each pursuit makes its own inner demands. If a man is to be a student and not a mere craftsman, he must be prepared to starve and sacrifice certain sides of his life, to let his energies get absorbed into one channel and concentrated on one interest. He must not mind becoming ' eccentric '; he need not feel astonished if he finds that, like the Athenian philosophers, ' he is not respected in our cities.' [2]

[1] Ruskin, *Modern Painters*, vol. iii, p. 224.
[2] Plato, *Republic*, Book VI, 489 A.

But it is true of the student of Pastoral Theology above all, from the intense interest of his subject, and from the fact that it enters into everything. He cannot be indifferent : he cannot escape the feeling which is described as a disease of modern society—namely, the restless sense of obligation to work, that comes when all round us seems to be moving and working.[1] He can only see to it that this sense of obligation is not forced ; that he does not become unbalanced, affected, priggish. He must learn to husband his resources so as to study and work with energy and concentration ; he must beware of condemning his fellow students as frivolous for an attitude that is often due to mere reaction or is assumed to unbend the bow. Only if he has an intense purpose can he stand the strain, and it still remains a real sacrifice that is demanded of him, a sacrifice of things often good in themselves, that are destroyed by a sense of seriousness, and by an obsession of the ideas that are necessary to the student of Pastoral Theology.

[1] Dante, *Purg.* iii. 10 :

> la fretta
> Che l' onestade ad ogni atto dismaga.

(The haste which mars the dignity of every act.)

CHAPTER III

THE LITERATURE OF PASTORAL THEOLOGY

WE have so far confined our attention almost exclusively to the Church of England and the study of Pastoral Theology in our own country. This is natural in a book written in English and by an English churchman. The subject is so great, and so little has been done to reduce it to order, that any effort must necessarily be tentative and limited. We can only write with any profit of what we know, and it is better to take a smaller canvas and fill it less inadequately than to confuse knowledge by accumulating details which cannot be ordered.

But there is another reason for deliberately adopting this narrower point of view. We have seen that the science of Pastoral Theology has yet to be constructed, and it would almost seem as if it could only be done by the Anglican Church. For to convert a study into a science two things are necessary—a sufficient area of observation and the spirit of free inquiry working through minds rightly trained. We still lack a satisfactory body of literature setting forth the results of the study of applied Christianity, and the Church of England has, at least, exceptional opportunities to produce it.

I

The litera-ture of Pastoral Theo-logy.

These two assertions would probably be con-troverted by most. They would argue that the Roman Church has inherited a vast mass of experience based on the observation of centuries ; that the activity of German Lutherans and of English and American Protestant bodies shows itself in the large and serious books on Practical Theology that they have issued ; and that, what-ever else may be wanting in our Church, there is no lack of literature on clerical work, for a con-tinuous stream of little books issues year by year from the publishers and shows no sign of abating.

In the Roman Church.

It need not be denied that the Roman Church inherits a priceless library from the past, or that this is ample, practical, based on tested evidence, and varied. We have only to look at the biblio-graphy at the beginning of such a book as Dr. J. B. Renninger's *Pastoraltheologie* [1] to be convinced of the fact. Even if we cannot allow the Roman Church to claim exclusive possession of the inheritance of patristic lore, she has full right to use it as her own. But the writings of the Fathers are rather materials for Pastoral Theology than works on it as a branch of Theology. Such set treatises as exist are occasional in origin, as, for

[1] *Pastoraltheologie.* Von Dr. J. B. Renninger. Heraus-gegeben von Dr. F. A. Göpfert, Freiburg i. B., Herder'sche Buchhandlung, 1893.

xample, the second Oration of Gregory of Nazianzus and Chrysostom's *De Sacerdotio*, or are, like Ambrose's *De Officiis*, based on a literary comparison with classic models rather than on direct personal observation. Augustine's *De Catechizandis Rudibus* speaks from first-hand experience, and is the product of a great mind, but it deals merely with one part of a priest's duties. Gregory's *De Cura Pastorali* aims at comprehensiveness, but reflects the standard and scope with which the Dark Ages had to be contented.

Practical needs, again, called out numerous sermons, letters, and catechetical addresses, which were presumably found useful to guide others in after-life, since they were copied and preserved. Especially was it found necessary to keep and codify the literature of Church government, the advice of Church Orders, and the decisions of Councils. Through the Dark and Middle Ages there was a real development in the compilation of Penitentiaries, and in rubrical direction, but Canon Law, Casuistry, and Liturgiology, though living studies in which much valuable work is being done, have only formed single departments of Pastoral Theology, which by Roman Catholic theologians has hardly been envisaged as a whole.

Again, the need of training the agents of applied Christianity has, no doubt, been faced in the Roman Church. The great developments of

Unscientific and mainly administrative.

Seminaries in the seventeenth century, the out
come of the decision of the Council of Trent, and
especially those connected with the names of Olier
and Vincent de Paul, compelled a thorough study
of a priest's calling, and ever since a continual
succession of minor works has appeared, dealing
with it in its various aspects.   Courses of study
have been mapped out, duties defined, and the
conception of the sacerdotal life seriously considered.   This literature is continually improving
in character, as witness, for instance, two such
recent works as Dr. T. B. Scannell's *The Priest's
Studies*,[1] and M. Charles Dementhon's admirable
Nouveau Mémento de Vie Sacerdotale.[2]   But rich
as is this inheritance of the Roman Church, excellent as are such special treatises, in spite of the
sense of completeness that their reading creates,
a continued study of them leaves us with a sense
of insufficiency and dryness.   The mass of patristic
and mediaeval literature dates from a pre-scientific
age, or at least from one in which the conception
of science was very different from ours, while the
admirable manuals of practical work are, after
all, mere administrative handbooks.   They in-

[1] *The Priest's Studies*, by T. B. Scannell, D.D. (Longmans,
Green & Co., 1908).

[2] *Nouveau Mémento de Vie Sacerdotale*, par l'Abbé Charles
Dementhon, 5ᵐᵉ édition (Paris: Beauchesne et Cie, 1907).
For a similar English book cp. *The Priest of To-day, His
ideals and duties*, by the Rev. Thomas O'Donnell, C.M.
(Brown & Nolan, Dublin, 1910).

truct us how a certain machine is worked; they apply only to one set of circumstances. It would seem, moreover, as if it were impossible for the Roman Church to get free from her tradition of one mental attitude, while experience drawn from the inner life of a body that aims at homogeneity is of little value to those outside, and certainly offers only one field of observation.

When we turn from Roman Catholic writers to those of the Protestantism in which German Lutherans take the lead, we find ourselves in a very different atmosphere. Among them, as among Presbyterians and Nonconformists at home, as well as among American Protestant writers, there is no lack of free inquiry, and no antagonism to the scientific spirit. In freedom, in sincerity, in thoroughness of method, there is little to be desired. Since the time of Schleiermacher, Practical Theology, as it is called in Germany, has been recognized as a separate science, and has received sufficient attention as such. A whole series of treatises has been issued, one after another, and a definite advance in the treatment of the subject can be marked. The two enormous volumes of Prof. E. C. Achelis' *Lehrbuch der praktischen Theologie*[1] show how thoroughly the

German Lutheran and Protestant Nonconformist.

---

[1] *Lehrbuch der praktischen Theologie.* Von Prof. Dr. E. Chr. Achelis. Zweite Auflage (Leipzig, J. C. Hinrich'sche Buchhandlung, 1898).

study has been carried on by students trained
in the most exhaustive and scientific school of
German method. Moreover, the clear conception
of the subject made possible by such separate
treatment is leading men to realize the defects of
current conceptions of pastoral duty, and the
enormous field still waiting for a fuller treatment.
Prof. Carl Clemen's *Zur Reform der praktischen
Theologie*,[1] the first number of a series of studies
in different departments of the subject, is a model
to illustrate the scientific attitude that is needed
for real advance.

Scienti-
fic but
of limi-
ted
scope.

Yet, withal, the whole is marred in the eyes of
an English churchman by a fatal defect. Admirable
as is the method, and full as is the treatment, the
area of observation is curiously narrow. Owing
to their training in a non-catholic Christianity,
the writers often confine their outlook to one
race, they rarely allude to any centuries between
the fifth and the fifteenth, they seem almost
unconscious of the existence of the Eastern, the
Roman, or the Anglican Churches. The Christianity of the school which they for the most part
represent now lays little stress on any body of
doctrine ; as a consequence they have little
theory of religious education. The sense of corporate life is feeble, so there is, as a rule, small

---

[1] *Studien zur praktischen Theologie*, Bd. I. 1. *Zur Reform
der praktischen Theologie*. Von Prof. Lic. Dr. Carl Clemen
(Giessen, A. Töpelmann, 1907).

nterest in questions of government or administration except in details.   No stress is laid on corporate worship, so the department of Liturgiology
almost disappears.   Mission work, with certain
noble exceptions, is in danger of being regarded
as mere extension, and the conception of growth,
consolidation, training, or deepening of spiritual
life, is hardly perceptible.   The idea of a ministerial
priesthood is absent, and the consequent narrowing of the whole scope of the science is borne
witness to by the name adopted.   Pastoral
Theology, the science of the work of man in helping
his fellow man in his relations to God, becomes
Practical Theology, and is largely coloured by
utilitarian aims.

As a consequence the main interest centres in
preaching.   On this subject there is an enormous
literature.   Much of it, in England and America
at least, is of the worst possible type.   Outline
sermons, preachers' aids, promptuaries of stories
for illustration, devices of all sorts for saving
trouble, are multiplied to make possible somehow
the enormous amount of preaching demanded.   And
even where the literature is good it is out of all
proportion to the rest.   Nor does the evil merely
lie in this disproportion ; the habit of sermonizing
is too often acquired, and betrays itself in what
should be scientific treatises.   The tendency to
perpetual 'edification' mars much of what is
written by this school.

The
Anglican
School
defects
and
oppor-
tunities.

We shall not get much direct help from either
Roman Catholic or Lutheran writers on Pastoral
Theology. But we can imitate the breadth of
view and the practical aims of the one class,
and the thoroughness and open-mindedness of the
other, while we can take warning by their defects
and set ourselves to do our own work independently. Nor have we any right to criticize them
except as a means of criticizing ourselves by comparison. We have not produced such good work
as they. We have hosts of little books, but few
serious treatises. Our conception of the science
is no clearer ; our ideas of church work no less
vague. We, too, have laid a disproportionate
stress on preaching, and have too often allowed
a 'preachy' tone to run through all we write. Much
that is said is irrelevant, much bears the stamp
of amateurishness. Much is occupied with mere
detail instead of ordering detail to illustrate great
principles. Much is merely a record of personal
experience or opinion, valuable as a single element
of evidence, but of no further worth. Many statements are put forth without being tested ; much
is slovenly and unreal. A low standard of attain-
ment and a poor ideal is often all that is upheld.
We have even more need than the Lutherans of
a ' reform of Practical Theology '.

But, in spite of all this, we have a better field
of work than any other body. Our conception of
Pastoral Theology is not limited to mere adminis-

tration, as in the over-organized Latin Church, and the administration that we have is of a type far more rich and varied. We have opportunities for experiment, and are not committed to any one system. Our Church is many-sided and our work in touch with many departments of life. We have by far the best field of observation. Moreover, as a Catholic body we inherit a tradition from the past, by our corporate life we can maintain a due proportion in the various parts of our work, for what one student does is balanced by the studies of another. Specialization loses its dangers when its agents form part of a body in touch with other activities and interests, and by our unity in one common life we are safeguarded from that over-elaboration of particular elements which is often the destruction of scientific work.

Our immediate need, therefore, is the adequate training of a body of students. As in ancient Athens, there is among us no little interest and much public talk, but there are too many sophists, and, as a consequence, there is no small measure of popular contempt. We want a Socrates to make us test our terms and analyse our facts. Or rather, we want what he advised, the educating of a body of young men as philosophers to be our rulers in the Church when they shall have attained to years of sufficient experience and discretion.

II

Anglican literature.

What materials have we at hand for the education of such a school of students ?   In the way of definite treatises, it must be confessed, very little that is of much value, but as standard text-books we have the good fortune to possess two works that rank among the great books of the world, which, moreover, have prevented the Pastoral Theology of the Church of England from sinking below a certain level, and have from their position as undisputed classics always remained for her a powerful instrument for revival and reform. These two works are the Book of Common Prayer and Hooker's *Ecclesiastical Polity*.

The Book of Common Prayer.

England had the rare chance to secure her Prayer Book before the confusion that, it would seem, was necessarily entailed by the Reformation. Cranmer, whatever his other qualities may have been, was a great translator. He was a translator not merely of Latin words into English, but of the Latin spirit into its counterpart in our race. He was in power at a cardinal point, and held together the old and the new. He possessed the liturgical sense that grows up with years of Catholic tradition and is hardly re-acquired by those who have not been born into it, while his work was practically completed before the crash came in which both traditional learning and liturgical sense were for so long destroyed.   The ew comparatively unimportant parts that were eft unfinished have remained incomplete ever since; the rubrics are still a source of confusion; the Burial Service remains a torso; where later hands have touched the book they have only weakened and disfigured it. We have thus a book thoroughly English, and one, therefore, able to be used during all these years, in varying developments of our society, and by men of very different types of mind; adaptable as are all great works, yet with a full Catholic tradition; able to respond to the revivals of the seventeenth and nineteenth centuries; never insular, appealing to the whole man, built up by the experience of ages, flexible in practical use, broad-based on human experience, and as such containing just what is necessary for scientific Pastoral Theology.

After the worst confusion of the Reformation was over Hooker appeared, a pastoral theologian of the first rank. It is true that his special pastoral field, that in which he was called on to help men spiritually, was the area of controversy. That was necessitated by the exigencies of the time. But he 'thought it convenient to wade through the whole cause, following that method which searcheth the truth by the causes of truth'.[1] He was, as Dean Church points out, 'one of those rare controversialists who are more intent on showing why their opponents are wrong than even the fact that

Hooker.

[1] Book V, *Epistle Dedicatorie*, § 3.

they are so, and who are not afraid of the challeng
to build as ₊well as destroy, or of the task of
replacing what they have refuted by a positive
construction which invites the test of a wide
application to facts.' [1]

His work has, that is, exactly the scientific
spirit ; he bases all he writes on laws, even finds
it necessary to begin by investigating the whole
nature of law, while his learning ensures these
laws being built up on wide generalizations from
tested evidence.   By the side of this it is a minor
point that, as in the case of the Prayer Book, his
language is a model which ' first revealed to the
nation what English prose might be ' ; his spirit
is essentially Anglican and his ideas curiously
modern.

An-
drewes
and
Laud.

Hooker's immense influence was seen later in
those who followed.   Andrewes is becoming more
and more recognized as typical of much that is
best in our Church.   His secret influence through
his *Devotions* is to-day enormous.   Laud's influence, on the other hand, was felt more immediately,
though for the full appreciation of the value of
his work we have had to wait till recent years.
In many ways it was characteristic of English
churchmanship, in his interest in social questions,
in the practical nature of his reforms, in the stress
he laid on matters of ritual—an emphasis generally
laid by way of objection to ceremonial—in his care

[1] Introduction to Hooker, Book I, p. xvi.   Oxford.

for the close association of the clergy with university life. But he was working against a strong body of opinion that was even more typically English, and so influenced by force and opposition rather than by interpreting the national character. Still none of these three men created a science of Pastoral Theology. Cranmer's work was the outcome of a trained sense of liturgical fitness ; Hooker's a model, but a single piece of scientific construction ; Laud's a practical experiment, but merely personal and empirical. Each provided materials, but a systematic theology was not deduced.

In George Herbert's *A Priest to the Temple, or Country Parson* (1632), we get the first work of English Pastoral Theology consciously written as such. It marks the beginning of a new school, and shows a complete break with tradition. The ideals of life, the circumstances and details, are all essentially those of our country. It is on right lines in that it begins by considering the agent ; for the first step needed is, as we saw, the training of the right type of student ; and it is based on first-hand observation and direct experience. But there the science stops. And when the conception of a parson is analysed, what does it amount to ? There is very little in his duty that is professional. He is to look after the church, but only a bare decency is required. He is to catechize, but there is no hint of any theory of education. He is to

George Herbert.

celebrate the Eucharist—at most once a month. He is to be ready to hear confessions, but evidently the practice is little observed. He is to visit, but apparently merely to give doles. The ideal is little more than that of a Christian gentleman,[1] the head of local society, but with few special duties, the professional good man, learned and courteous, who, where he tries to be more, feels himself in a false position and is fearful of becoming a bore, frankly bribing people to come to church. We gather an impression of the Country Parson as a lovable and devout man, of a type we all know and are the better for knowing. But there is very little substance in the conception of his duty. His life is meagre, poor, vague, isolated ; his methods casual and promiscuous. The book contributes just one item of experience, direct, but merely personal.

Gilbert Burnet.

With Burnet's *Discourse of the Pastoral Care* (1692) we enter a new atmosphere. His is the

---

[1] Cf. Preface to the Reader by Barnabas Oley in his second edition. ' The advantage of doing God service, which height of birth gives to a nobleman or gentleman, over what a clerk of lower parentage hath, is very considerable. The truth taught by them is sooner believed ; a reproof bestowed by them is better received ; an example of virtue shewed by them makes deeper impression than the same coming from one of meaner extraction would do. This observation I first made in those two great lights of our church, Dr. Fern, Lord Bishop of Chester, who was a knight's son, and Dr. Hammond, who was of an ancient family. And the reader will observe more in this book, whose author was a person nobly descended.'

earliest English work that aims at being a special and full treatise on Pastoral Theology. The idea of the work was suggested by Gregory's *De Cura Pastorali*, and there was a closer parallel in circumstances, in the attitude and qualifications of the writer, and in the conditions of contemporary church life, than he probably realized. If it cannot be said to have founded a school, it greatly influenced later writers both in England and abroad.[1] It was planned as a whole, is ordered and complete, the work of a comprehensive and powerful mind. Moreover, the treatment of the subject is on right lines. After emphasizing his dissatisfaction with the prevailing type of church work (all works on Pastoral Theology seem to make the same complaint in every age), Burnet examines the fundamental nature of the clerical calling, tracing its ideals from those found in the New Testament, through the course of history down to its special English development ; then he considers the primary question of practical efficiency, namely, the training and preparation needed for the ministry, with a full working out of various branches of necessary study, and finally considers the duties of a parish priest point by point.

The scheme is admirable in conception, but when we come to examine it in detail we cannot help being struck with the poverty of its ideal. The activities of the priest are confined to mere personal

[1] Cp. Vinet, *Théologie Pastorale* [E. T.], ch. i, p. 20.

and individual efforts ; his duties amount to little more than preaching, excellent advice about which fills nearly all the pages devoted to practical work. The clergyman is no more than a sort of moral policeman in the parish. The whole is quite out of sympathy with real life, for it is a seventeenth-century bishop's charge to his diocese. He speaks all through *de haut en bas*. He obviously moves in a different world from that of his clergy, and so is doubly removed from the spiritual life of the people. The treatise resolves itself into another expression of a purely individual opinion, an opinion of an exceptionally able man, no doubt, but of one who has taken no pains to find out what even his clergy think. The style is the natural outcome of his attitude, pompous and preachy, wearisome in its rolling phrases and utterly unreal—and yet, withal, so English.

Later writers.

Later writers abound, but they carry on the same tradition. They adopt almost invariably the standpoint of Herbert or Burnet. They either give a single piece of individual experience, or speak unreally and with condescension. Baxter's *Reformed Pastor* (1655) contains a valuable account of the way in which he established catechizings in his parish, but the rest is mere words. Jeremy Taylor, who was not a conspicuous success in the parish, gives in his *Rules and Advice to the Clergy* (1661) a series of general precepts written with all his peculiar charm, but containing for the most part merely the sort of counsel a man can give equally well to himself. It is the prototype of a whole family of later little books of edification. Bishop Wilson's *Parochialia or Instruction to the Clergy on the Discharge of their Parochial Duty* (1708) is excellent, practical, and detailed, but it is a bishop's charge delivered autocratically to his clergy. It speaks from experience, but reveals no patient spirit of inquiry. Bishop Spratt, in his *Visitation Discourse to the Clergy of the Diocese of Rochester* (1695), takes eight pages to tell them to say their office daily, and enjoins it as excellent practice in reading which will improve their delivery of sermons ! Bishop Bull, in his *Visitation Sermon and Charge, A Companion for the Candidate for Holy Orders, or the Great Importance of the Priestly Office* (1714), embellishes his oratory with Hebrew, Latin, and Greek quotations, but contents himself with generalities ; while Bishop Gibson, in his *Directions to the Clergy of the Diocese of London,* issued in 1724, and in his *Charge* of 1742, if slightly more practical and a little less oratorical, emphasizes quite elementary conventional clerical duties. Nor are Bishop Hort's *Instructions to the Clergy of the Diocese of Tuam given at his Primary Visitation* (1742) any more helpful, they merely repeat the traditional advice usually given on such occasions.

The above, with the exception of Baxter's *Reformed Pastor,* were collected and published by the Delegates of the Oxford Clarendon Press in 1807, under the title of *The Clergyman's Instructor*. This 'Collection of Tracts on the Minister's Duties' was frequently reprinted, and new editions appeared at intervals during the next fifty years. It may therefore be taken as representing fairly the official and dominant conception of Pastoral Theology through the eighteenth and early nineteenth centuries. The Evangelical revival no doubt introduced a new spirit of earnestness and added a new element of missionary activity; the Tractarian movement made a new note sound in its more spiritual conception of the priestly office; the industrial change brought about a development of parochial work by shifting the centre of English life to the towns; but the stock remains essentially the same, and can be easily recognized as the foundation of writings of the great mid-Victorian period such as those of Liddon or Blunt. The new enthusiasm works on the old lines. The deeper devotion is but grafted on, and the new developments of practical work are mere extensions of country methods to utterly changed conditions.

Modern writers.
It would be invidious to particularize in speaking of the more modern type of manual of Pastoral Theology.[1] The books written are almost all on

[1] A useful list will be found in the new Schaff-Herzog *Encyclopedia of Religious Knowledge*, vol. viii, p. 379, Art. 'Pastoral Theology'.

the same lines, though the language is more modern. The same complaints are made, the same abuses (with the exception of non-residence) remain unreformed. The same methods are advised ; the same emphasis is laid on preaching. The books alternate between the relating of individual personal experiment, and the repetition of academic or episcopal ideals, valuable and inspiring, but in no way scientific. The conception of the duties of the priest has never really got free from the alternative of that of the moral policeman (whether 'squarson' or superintendent of boys' clubs), or that of the professional good man who is not to be too different from a layman.

To sum up, we have the advantage of possessing two great literary works—a liturgy in the vernacular, necessarily influencing all we do, with possibilities of development all the greater, perhaps, from the fact that neglect has at least kept us free from an inflexible tradition, and a standard work of theology treating fundamentally most of our characteristic features of church life. We have a tradition of learning and culture, of a clergy in touch with national life, accustomed to take part in all sorts of social movements, ready to be influenced by current thought. The weakness of our organization at least allows us freedom to try new methods ; our Catholic tradition has kept a framework to hold these together ; and practical duties stand in no danger of being neglected.

III

The national ideal.

What is wanted, then, to build up a national ideal ? What is needed to make the general conception of the work scientific ? The first step in scientific process is to define the subject considered. The work is then seen as a whole and in relation to other sciences. When it has been defined, its various parts may be examined in proportion to one another and in their mutual relationships. This will best be done by considering the agent in Pastoral Theology. For in his personality the various departments of pastoral work find their connexion, and when a clear four-square ideal of clerical work has been traced out the training of the student will be directed to a definite end. The diversity of his functions can best be examined as correlated in a single individual, and the subjects of a school can then be elaborated with less fear of their becoming academic and losing touch with real life. We want to retain the personal first-hand element of church work, with its scope for the full realization of the parson's individuality against the somewhat mechanical conception (as it seems to us) of the Roman Catholic priesthood, and to maintain the proportion and balance of his duties as against the one-sided development of Evangelical Protestantism.

BOOK II

THE AGENT IN PASTORAL THEOLOGY

' Ego tamen Deo nostro gratias ago, quod in his quatuor libris, non qualis ego essem, cui multa desunt, sed qualis esse debeat, qui in doctrina sana, id est, Christiana, non solum sibi sed etiam aliis laborare studet, quantulacumque potui facultate disserui.'—AUG. *De Doct. Christ.* Lib. IV, c. xxxi.

(I thank God that in these four books I have set forth as well as I can—not what I am myself, for I come short in much, but—what a man should be who tries to labour in sound, that is Christian, doctrine, not for himself but for others.)

CHAPTER I

THE WORK OF A CLERGYMAN

WHAT exactly is the work of an English clergy-man ? The first step in the scientific study of any subject is to define its scope ; therefore before we can hope to make our Pastoral Theology more thorough and effective we must have a clear idea what it is that a clergyman has to do. We have many little treatises advising him how to do it, and perhaps still more dealing with the necessary qualifications for his calling—it is so simple to publish Ordination addresses—but hardly any that begin by considering what his work is. Many of those who are working the hardest would

E 2

find it very difficult to answer the question in the light of hard cross-questioning by a businesslike layman, or to take pen and paper and put down simply and clearly what his duties are.   And in truth few of us know.   We have certain vague conventional ideas which are the product of a sentimental Romanticism, but the stage priest and the parson of the ordinary novel, whether caricatured or idealized, bear little resemblance to anything in real life.   Our biographies of heroes of the slums are written up in the uncritical style of the lives of the Saints.

Disillu-
sion-
ment
from
lack of
a clear
ideal.

The consequence is a widespread disillusionment which overtakes the newly ordained.   It does not arise from difficulties in their work.   These were expected.   Moreover, the great disillusionment is not felt at first just because of these little worries. Things never do turn out just as we had hoped. But if we have the steadfast purpose that comes from a clear ideal we can fight through obstacles. Difficulties overcome are an actual help, and we enjoy them.   A large part of the pleasure of life is due to the mastering of troubles, and, in any case, if we have a set purpose we can be patient.   If the whole wide issue is seen in each immediate detail we can be content with an inferior position.   We do not 'expect Plato's Republic' at once.   We see how one part of the work helps the whole, that none stands alone, and that we must begin somewhere. But after a year or two the newly ordained clergyman begins to realize that the difficulties are greater and more fundamental than he thought, and it is because most have no clear ideal that, after the bewilderment of the first rush—generally at about the end of two years—they are at a loss and discouraged. We want, therefore, to forestall this, to consider in detail and as a whole what exactly is the work of a clergyman.

The clergy, according to the English conception of their office, are Ministers of the Word and Sacraments. They unite in themselves the functions of prophet and priest, though, as individuals, in different proportions. One side of the work attracts one man more than another. Just as some men are better at theory and some at practice, some at initiative and some at administration, so clergymen tend to form themselves into parties or schools of thought and group themselves as Catholic or Evangelical as they are attracted more to the work of the priest or to that of the prophet. The two conceptions are not antagonistic but complementary. While it is a good thing for individuals as specialists to be of one class or the other, the Church as a whole must be balanced and comprehensive.

In order of time the prophet comes before the priest, at any rate in a new movement. So Moses preceded Aaron ; the priestly development of the religion of Israel was later than the prophetic, even though the law was given by Moses. Ezra organized, and so preserved, the work that Isaiah had initiated. So St. Paul of necessity preached first, and then ordained elders. Historically the episcopate arose out of the apostolic mission. The primitive prophets soon died out, and Montanism was not a survival of an earlier Christianity but a reactionary innovation.[1]

But though pioneer trading comes before business, in an already established commercial world the process is reversed. Office work and method are learned first, and many are of necessity employed in them all their lives. Others, after they have been trained in the regular machinery of trade, go out as travellers to extend the connexion of their house. So in the spiritual commerce of a Christian country, in an organized and established church, the administration of the Sacraments, the office of a priest, comes first. The ideas are distinct ; the agents, and to a great extent the methods, are one.

I

Minister of the Sacraments : (1) Baptism.
The priest as Minister of the Sacraments is the responsible agent in the celebration of Baptism and of the Eucharist, the two great Sacraments of the Gospel according to the definition of the English Church. The one is the rite of admission into the

---

[1] For an opposite view see Hatch, *The Organization of the Early Christian Churches*, Bampton Lectures, 1880, p. 120.

Body, the other the central act of common worship and the chief means of grace to individuals.

The ministration of Baptism, therefore, involves the whole question of church government. The existence of the Sacrament implies a social as well as an individual conception of Christianity. The clergy are not, that is to say, mere sacrificing priests, or spiritual physicians, but are charged with the administration of a corporate body. Their work is, in part, that of government officials in a spiritual kingdom, and corresponds with that of civil servants in a secular polity.

A Governor.

The analogy is an important one, as it involves three points in the theory of government, which in their turn are of practical moment in the relationship of priest to people. The clergyman is the representative and servant or minister of the people, but he acts with constitutional authority. Neither can do anything without the other. The priest cannot exercise his functions without a congregation ; without a bishop there is no church. So the priest can neither rule arbitrarily, ' lording it over God's heritage ' ; nor, though he is their servant, is he the creature of the people. The conception is one with which we are quite familiar in civil government and is the Catholic theory of the Church of England, but many people find it difficult to grasp because the despotic and military theory of Romanism, and the demagogic theory of Protestant Nonconformity, are presented to them so clearly that they find it hard to oppose to each a theory of constitutional liberty. Thus while all authority is from the bishop, in the sense that he represents the continuous Church and delegates his power to the clergy, still, according to the English conception of government— a conception as old as the days of King Alfred— the constitutional ruler is the servant and representative of the people, not their lord.[1]

Baptism and God-parents.

The parish priest may be compared to the secretary of a local branch of a club, part of whose duty it is to see to the admission of new members in accordance with the rules of the whole body. Though the act of Baptism gives new birth and admission into a Catholic society, Grace received is not effective merely *ex opere operato*. The new life can only germinate in the right soil, just as membership of a club only becomes a real thing when the elected share in its social life. He cannot, therefore, baptize indiscriminately. An official responsibility in this matter rests with him.[2]

God-parents.

It is his duty to see after the number and status of the godparents, just as the secretary has to see, or write to, the referees given by an applicant for admission. The responsibility for admission, as

[1] Cp. R. C. Moberly, *Ministerial Priesthood*, especially chaps. iii and iv.

[2] Cp. *The Spiritual Efficiency of the Church* : the Primary Charge delivered at his Visitation to the Clergy and Church-wardens of his Diocese by Charles Gore, D.D., Bishop of Worcester, October 1904 (Murray), pp. 38 ff.

distinct from that of seeing that the necessary
conditions are fulfilled, rests primarily on the
other members of the body. In clubs a proposer
and seconder from those who are already members
is usually demanded. The Church of England
demands three communicant godparents. The
proposer and seconder in a club must, as a rule,
be persons not related to the new candidate
for election ; in the Church the sponsors must
normally be persons other than the parents of the
child who is to be made one of the ' elect people
of God '. In exceptional cases, where the applicants are unknown to the older members of the
club, outside references are demanded, and the
proposers and seconders act *pro forma* ; so it is
legitimate for the clergyman to accept sponsors
who are communicants but are quite uncon-
nected with the persons to be baptized, provided
that they have satisfied themselves by inquiry
from referees (who need not necessarily be churchmen) as to their moral fitness. If the club has
relaxed its care in ' taking up ' outside references
of applicants for admission, or has lowered its
standard, and is suffering in consequence, it is the
duty of the secretary gradually to string up its
discipline, and to be growing continually more
strict in demanding fulfilment of the recognized
conditions. This is a perfectly definite and intelligible kind of work, one with which we are all
familiar, and recognized as part of an occupation

suitable for a man of initiative and character. In the same way, to raise the standard of sponsorship for Baptism till it is understood that sponsors must be communicants, is part of a clergyman's work. To do so demands a clear policy gradually and steadily carried out ; it will involve a great amount of detailed work both in visiting and writing letters, but its spiritual effect will reach far beyond what we can see.[1]

Confirmation.

Confirmation is part of the rite of Baptism ; in England it is reserved for administration by the bishop in person, and deferred to an age at which it is considered that the privileges of full membership in the Church can be appreciated, and its responsibilities accepted. The analogy of initiation of juvenile members into an adult Court of a Friendly Society is a close one. The responsibility of presenting to the bishop rests with the priest as Minister of Baptism, that of preparing, or arranging for preparation, with the godparents. But since it is always more difficult, though more effective, to see that others do their work than to do it for them, the majority of the clergy both prepare and examine, as well as present, the candidates, often without even consulting the godparents. The preparation and examination are naturally insufficient, and the present methods, even where conscientiously carried out, are generally felt to be

[1] For a suggestion as to the practical methods of carrying it out see my *Principles of Parish Work*, pp. 133 ff.

a stumbling-block. Again here is need for steady and persistent efforts for reform. As Minister of the Word, it is no doubt, as we shall see, the clergyman's duty to instruct the candidates, or to arrange for their instruction, but as Minister of Baptism it is his duty to throw back the responsibility of fulfilling their promises on the godparents, and to test the knowledge and religious habits of those who apply to be presented to the bishop for Confirmation.[1] This, again, will involve a large amount of definite straightforward work in visiting, writing, examining, and interviewing, all of which, if conscientiously done, will involve incalculable spiritual effects.

As Minister of Baptism the priest is the responsible officer for the after fulfilment of its conditions by those who wish to share in its privileges. He has to deal with those who, by not fulfilling them, have lapsed from active membership and have forfeited their rights. This ministry of reconciliation is different from that of conversion, which is part of his duties as Minister of the Word. It may be formalized into a definite tribunal, as is done universally in the Roman Church, in which case he will hear confessions and grant absolution ; a function quite different from that of giving direction, though often associated with it. By the Church of England, however, in her official documents, private confession is regarded in its

Restoration of the lapsed.

[1] Cp. my *Principles of Parish Work*, pp. 137 ff.

aspect of a remedy for sin and a means of grace for the individual, as a voluntary and exceptional act, rather than as a condition of restoration for the lapsed ; and to hear confessions when called upon to do so may more properly be reckoned as part of the function of a priest as Minister of the Eucharist than of Baptism.

As the official empowered to receive applications for reinstatement in the Church, his duty is to be acquainted with the conditions necessary in each case, to explain them to applicants, and to see that they are fulfilled. Naturally, he will also give them all the help he can to do what is necessary. This would seem to involve work like that of the director of an inquiry office or that of a consulting physician. The priest should be accessible at certain hours, not, like St. Ambrose, in his private house [1] where the surroundings are those of ordinary social life, where the bell has to be rung for admittance, and names are asked even if an introduction is not considered necessary, but in an open church. It should be part of the duties of a clergyman to be in the church as in an office (not in a secluded vestry) at certain definite hours. Here he could explain to those who had lapsed the steps they must take for reinstatement, to those coming from another parish how they can be transferred to the organizations of the new, to those desiring to be received from another com-

[1] Cp. Augustine, *Confessions,* Book VI, ch. iii.

munion exactly what they must do. Here, too,
he, with his staff, could deal with the various details
of administration which need a centre, keeping up
the roll of members, transferring them when they
leave the district, writing commendatory letters,
or receiving official visits.

The priest has to see that the privileges of the Mar-
Church are available for those who fulfil its con- riages.
ditions. Thus, for instance, he puts the questions
and makes the statements that guarantee a
Christian marriage, and, as the official representative of the Church, blesses the union after the
bride and bridegroom have married with one
another. He is responsible for the fulfilment of
the proper conditions beforehand ; he publishes
the banns, and explains the nature of Christian
marriage. He is under the obligation, on putting
up the banns, of seeing that his parishioner under-
stands the responsibility and purpose of matrimony
and that the couple are qualified to be married
as members of the Church. He has to uphold
the law of the Church as to the indissolubility of
wedlock, and as to the impossibility of marrying
relations by marriage of the first degree, against
the law of the land. Questions of anticipated,
and of mixed, marriages also come within his
jurisdiction.

So again with regard to funerals, he has to Funer-
decide who by her rules are entitled to the als.
services of the Church, in what cases the life or

action of the deceased forbids the Prayer Book
Office being used, what substitutes can be used
for suicides, for the unbaptized, or for persons
of evil life, whether it should be used for non-
communicants, or what additions can be made
(music, celebrations of the Eucharist, &c.) for those
who have died in the communion of the Church.

'Parish Work.'

All these are questions of administration, and
with them may be included all the whole government of a parish, the creation and calling of
councils, the associating of various members of the
Church in work. The priest, or staff of clergy,
is the meeting-point or clearing-house of parish
activities. All the business of parish management
centres in him as minister of the body of baptized ;
matters of finance, keeping of records, organization, committees, superintendence of subordinates,
use of volunteers, adaptation to special conditions,
all the external framework of social Christianity,
first in the parish and then in the diocese, are for
him to see to. All this that has been enumerated
is involved in the conception of the clergyman
as Minister of Baptism, and represents one-third,
or rather, since as Minister of the Word he must
also be a student, one-quarter of his work.

II

(2) As Minister of the Eucharist.

As Minister of the second great Gospel Sacrament
the priest has to do with the Eucharist both as the
chief and central act of common worship, and as

a means of grace to the individual. He has, that is, to celebrate the Lord's Supper and to administer the Communion. But in these two duties are involved all questions of the corporate expression of Christian life, as well as those of individual spiritual help to Christian souls. This is the side of the priest's work that has been more prominent in history; as certain of the lesser orders grew up round the Sacrament of Baptism and administration has tended to be gathered into the hands of bishops, so the work of the priest himself has tended to become centred round, and even almost confined to, the altar.[1]

As the official representative of the worshipping Church the priest's work is to say and sing her Offices. He does this as one of the community, as their mouthpiece, not instead of them; if he is a mediator between God and man he is not a substitute for either to either. This is emphasized in two apparently contradictory customs by the two great schools of the English Church; the one laying stress on the Eastward Position in celebrating the Sacrament to mark the fact that the priest stands at the altar as one of the congregation; the other insisting on the North End position no less strenuously to prevent his being regarded as separate from them. *Public worship.*

In addition to her Sunday worship, the Church as a whole keeps up a round of praise and prayer *The Daily Office.*

[1] Cp. R. C. Moberly, *Ministerial Priesthood*, ch. vii, pp. 220 ff.

in her morning and evening Offices, and the priest is charged with maintaining this. Where possible he has to say them publicly ; in any case he is bound to say them privately.[1] The idea is not that he is more holy and so more likely to be heard, an essentially pagan theory, or that he is bound to set an example, an idea based on the 'professional good man' conception of his calling, but that he, as the official representative, must keep up the chain into which private observance by individuals and broken attendance of the laity may be linked.

Care of the church.

The work of a clergyman as Minister of Public Worship involves the whole question of the methods by which it is conducted. He has to train himself both in reading and singing till he has such control of his voice as will enable him to put personal expression into the words he utters when it is demanded, or to keep it out when it would be unseemly ; obviously his intonation and delivery must be different when he is preaching and when leading Common Prayer in which all join with the voice. It involves thought about a whole host of practical details and care in carrying them out, about all the matters which correspond to office routine in business ; such are details concerning administration of the Elements, of ritual, of care of the altar, of carrying out

[1] Cp. *The Book of Common Prayer.* 'Concerning the Service of the Church.'

liturgical rubrics, of order in the sacristy, of discipline in the vestry, of kneeling accommodation, of choir practices, of organ-tuning, of choosing of hymns, &c., &c., all the things which do not concern laymen and bore them so intensely when discussed, which nevertheless need careful thought and supervision just because they are so unimportant in themselves that they must not be allowed to go wrong and to distract people's attention from things that matter. In attending to these he must keep in mind the larger issues which they help or hinder. Just as a librarian can exercise great influence on his readers by the preparation of his catalogue, by securing easy accessibility of the books under his charge, by enforcing the discipline that ensures comfort, and insisting on fresh air and quiet in his reading-room, so the priest can help his congregation by careful attention to all that goes on in his church. He may either feel obliged to maintain a ritual that the congregation wants because he sees that it is the real expression of their devotion, or be constrained to go against their desires because they are members of a greater body governed by general principles of self-expression ; but his action must be reasoned and scientific ; he must not do merely what he himself likes, but must maintain what on psychological grounds are found to be true expressions of Christian worship. Even more important than the ritual and ornaments of the chancel is the tone of the church, which is created partly by external circumstances—seating, hours of service, lighting, decoration, cleanliness, ventilation, accessibility out of service time, reverence on the part of officials—and partly, but in a far greater degree, by his own personality and example.   Care for all these is part of his work as Minister of the Eucharist.

The mouth-piece of Christian opinion.

In this capacity the priest is also the official representative of the Church in her activities other than worship, both to her members and to those outside.   He has to be the official voice of public Christian opinion, as a secretary of a club writes in the name of his committee.   He must feel the pulse of public life to learn what is its state, and must aim at having ready the Christian answer to its questions.   He must translate into definitely Christian terms all that is implicitly Christian in the phrases of the non-ecclesiastical world.   Still more must he be the voice of the Christian consciousness to the Christian community itself, focusing and clarifying its beliefs by clear presentation of them in the pulpit and elsewhere.   The value of pointed speech in clearing ideas and stimulating purpose among those who are at one can hardly be over-estimated.   This involves one aspect of preaching, roughly that of the morning sermon, which is quite different from that which has evangelization for its aim.   The one, according to our definition, is included in the function of the clergyman as Minister of the Eucharist, the other is part of his duty as Minister of the Word.

Finally, this part of a clergyman's work involves what, by a curious limitation of its meaning to units instead of to the flock, is generally understood by his ' pastoral' duties. The priest must be a minister to individuals. Here, again, he is their servant rather than their master. As the English conception of a policeman is not, for ordinary men, that of a man to keep you in order, but of one to help you in your difficulties—a conception that makes our ' men in blue ' the envy of the world, and, moreover, works extremely well—so the priest, if he is to be considered a sort of moral policeman, must be the helper and guide of his people ; he must get into touch with them, but only in quite exceptional cases need he ' get hold of them '. He must learn to see and to point out the Christian issues in all questions, to know how to give directions in difficulties and to answer the questions of the puzzled ; he must be able to refer men to books to be read or authorities to be consulted. As a C.O.S. secretary aims at being in touch with all the sources of material help available for a case of distress, and is accessible in his office for that purpose, so the priest's business is to be in touch with the various sources of spiritual help and to be no less accessible. By continual experience of being consulted he will gradually learn to speak with authority, if only he sets

Ministration to individuals.

himself to notice religious phenomena, to observe what helps people spiritually and what does not, what are the special needs of the young and the old, of the educated and the uneducated, of men and women, of the simple and the strong, and what are the best methods to meet them.

The functions of the clergyman as Minister of the Sacraments and of the Word overlap, both actually because his work in one capacity helps that of the other, and also in their nature. The mission work of the Church is bound up with her spiritual health ; administrative work done well is mission work. By the law of growth the removal of hindrances and careful service, weeding as well as St. Paul's planting and Apollo's watering, result in God giving the increase. That is, the clergyman as priest is primarily an official and an administrator, but he is not a mere official. This is guaranteed by the fact that he is also a Minister of the Word.

III

As Minister of the Word.   As Minister of the Word a clergyman is a preacher of the Gospel. It is his business to convert individuals, to extend the borders of the Church, to declare her doctrines, to spread the jurisdiction of her moral law, and to intensify her spiritual life. This is the evangelical and aggressive aspect of his work complementary to the catholic, and consolidating, side.

In this capacity he is called upon to 'preach' Preach-
in the technical sense. He has to deliver sermons ing.
from the pulpit to outsiders, to those who sit loosely
to religion, to nonconformist church-goers, and
to the whole class of person which corresponds to
that of the catechumen in the fourth century, who
often, like St. Augustine, for years, sometimes even
during his whole life, made no advance towards
baptism. To such the Sunday evening sermon
is generally addressed, while that delivered to the
morning congregation assumes a preponderance
of practising Christians. Thus while, according to
our definition, the latter forms part of the Ministry
of the Sacraments, the former is more properly
speaking preaching as part of the Ministry of the
Word. But of this kind of preaching the forms
are various ; different places and types of congregation call for different styles. Homiletical
work includes addresses to children, mission
sermons and courses, open-air work, and the
conducting of revivals, even though the methods
by which these are carried on may sometimes be
open to criticism.

But the effect and permanent value of such
preaching, great as it may be, has probably been
exaggerated. From the evidence of history and
from the present experience of foreign missions it
would appear that it is only one factor among
many, and probably not the most powerful,
in the expansion of Christianity. Certainly the

emphasis laid on the one method by the English Church has caused other methods of propaganda to be comparatively neglected by clergymen who limit their conception of evangelical duty to mere preaching.

Religious education.

Foremost among these other methods is that of religious education. It is an integral part of a clergyman's work to teach in schools. His duty under this head is not fulfilled by mere taking part in supplementary, or amateur, teaching such as that given in Sunday Schools, Bible or Confirmation classes. Religion should be an essential part of education and not a mere extra subject. Secular or undenominational education is, of course, a thing possible, but it differs *in toto* from religious education. Nor is it only in elementary schools that the clergy are bound to teach ; it is their work to give religious instruction in secondary and public schools, in Universities, Training and Theological Colleges, or at University Extension centres, as part of an all-round education of the whole man. Supplementary teaching and independent lecturing through special societies or Home Reading Unions is a part of their work which calls loudly for organization and development. Just as the great problem of Agriculture in England is not that of production but of markets and distribution,[1] as the work of the

[1] Cp. A. G. L. Rogers, *The Business Side of Agriculture* (Methuen, 1904).

middleman in creating wealth is in point of value greater than that of manufacture, so the splendid theological work of our English Universities needs to be retailed to the masses all over the country, and for lack of special travelling Ministers of the Word lies to a great extent unused at the centres of production. Still, after all, it is the Christian character of the normal education of the people that must first be secured, and for this the clergy must take part in school teaching.

But mere instruction is only a part of education. The life of the school and its relation to the home and to the district is an essential factor in the development of the whole child. It is therefore the work of a clergyman to take part in the management of the school and to connect it with home and parish life. In this way he can back up the efforts of the schoolmaster, and secure to the education of the school the broader, more liberal and humane, character that only the catholic religion of the Incarnation can supply. The duties of a manager in a Church school, or in looking after the Church children in a mixed school, are essentially those of a clergyman as Minister of the Word, and with them is bound up the duty of the clergy to consider the whole question of Christian education, its aims and methods, and, in co-operation with the laity, to formulate a practical policy to secure it. It is their business to become experts in the matter of moral and religious upbringing, and for this they must gather the experience of those actually engaged in teaching as their profession, who must, for the most part, always be laymen.

Foreign missions.

Foreign, as distinct from home, missionary work is also part of the work of the clergy, and, though generally considered as a branch by itself and undertaken by specialists, it has its close analogies with home work as well as its own peculiar difficulties. It is mainly carried on by the two methods of preaching and teaching, though they are rendered more difficult by differences of custom, language, and civilization. As at home, much of the most sure advance is made by unconscious growth (as notably in South India) in surroundings made favourable to religious life by diligent discharge of duties connected with the Ministry of the Sacraments. Probably missions have suffered by having the differences of condition and method over-emphasized, and certainly home work would profit by experience from the foreign mission field. Whilst the work of a foreign missionary is that of a specialist in propaganda, that of the normal clergyman as Minister of the Word includes keeping up the connexion between the two, not merely in order to raise financial support, but for the interchange between the one and the other of experience in the work of expansion.

Again, certain interests and needs are best Special.
furthered by special societies. The work of Temper- interests
ance or of Purity, of promotion of Christian Knowledge, of extension by subdivision of parishes, of
church building, of the increase of the Episcopate,
of Church Reform or Defence, of the supply and
training of candidates for Orders, &c., &c., may
all be considered as elements in the spread of
the Church, and the advocacy of their claims, or
performance of the office duties in connexion with
the societies created for their furtherance, may
be regarded as part of the Ministry of the
Word and, as such, as part of the work of a
clergyman.

But the influence of the Church is not spread Personal
merely by word of mouth. It is the experience of influence.
all who are engaged in political propaganda or in
education that other factors play a large part in
growth of movements or forces. The personality
of a speaker or organizer, distribution of literature,
and, before all, the careful formulation of policy,
are more potent than the mere spoken words.

Hence to exert personal influence is the work of
a clergyman. How this may be done, how far any
particular method is successful, healthy, or permanent in its result, is often a difficult matter to
decide. It may be that it should be deliberately
exerted and that the clergyman should endeavour,
by diligent ' house to house ' or social visiting to
make himself acceptable to the people that he

comes across, and so to 'break down prejudice' against the institution he represents ; or it may be that such action has exactly the opposite effect and that unconscious influence, both in the pulpit and in society, is the only kind that is of any force. It may be wise to create special organizations where the clergyman may make his influence felt and to invite people to come and be influenced, in which case a large part of his work will consist of superintendence of boys' and men's clubs ; or he may consider that this is a singularly costly and clumsy way of getting into touch with a few people, and that it is only in conscientious fulfilling of natural duties that character makes itself felt, and will prefer to devote what time he can spare to public service, it may be as Guardian or Councillor or in taking office in Friendly Society work, and there try to make the influence of the Church felt in a natural and legitimate manner.

Social duty.

Some social connexion between the different members of the congregation must exist, and some attitude towards the work of Charity and Social Reform must be adopted. It may be that the borders of the Church are extended by practical benevolence, or it may be that both depth of spirituality and increase in numbers depend on demands being made on people's best selves. According as the clergyman holds the one view or the other, will his work vary. Either it will consist largely in administration of relief, ' doing good to those of the household of faith,' [1] and in organizing innumerable treats and teas as rewards for the performance of religious duties ; or he will think that this is no part of his work and will urge people to give their alms carefully and thoughtfully with no respect for religious profession, and to pay for, and manage, their amusements for themselves. But, speaking generally, it may be safely assumed that it is strength of character, rather than a weak desire for popularity, that has power, and that this is often greatest where, exercised unconsciously and not paraded, it tells all through the organization of any institution. The official representative of the Church is always on duty in England, and often where he least suspects it his influence is felt ; hence the importance of good manners, dress, cleanliness, civility, and naturalness, as opposed to an affected clericalism or, worse, an affected secular geniality ; [2] care for all these things is part of his work.

The work of propaganda is also carried on by literature, and though this method is little developed in England, to make use of it is essentially part of the duties of a preacher in the larger sense. Public opinion is probably to-day formed

Propaganda by literature.

---

[1] Misapplied from Gal. vi. 10.

[2] Cp. Boswell's *Life of Johnson* (1781) : ' Even the dress of a clergyman should be in character and nothing can be more despicable than conceited attempts at avoiding the appearance of the clerical order, attempts which are as ineffectual as they are pitiful.'

far more by books, and by the press, than by the pulpit.[1] All literary work, therefore—improvement of the Parish Magazine and of religious publications generally, writing for the Church, local, or general press, distribution of tracts and leaflets, management of Parish Theological Libraries (whether in connexion with Reading Circles or Sunday School Teachers' classes, or independently), posting of placards, correcting misstatements in the newspapers, localizing Church periodicals and aiding their circulation, writing, lending, or distributing popular, apologetic, and other pamphlets, all offer to the clergy a field for intelligent missionary activity.

Politics. It is generally agreed that the clergy should not take sides publicly in party politics. On the other hand, there are many social questions in which, possibly, they are called upon to give voice to the Christian conscience. Perhaps, too, it may be right to form political organizations apart from party to look after exclusively Church interests

---

[1] Cp. R. L. Stevenson, *Essays in the Art of Writing.* II. The Morality of the Profession of Letters : 'Every article, every piece of verse, every essay, every *entre-filet*, is destined to pass, however swiftly, through the minds of some portion of the public, and to colour, however transiently, their thoughts. When any subject falls to be discussed, some scribbler on paper has the invaluable opportunity of beginning its discussion in a dignified and human spirit ; and if there were enough who did so in our public press, neither the public nor the parliament would find it in their minds to drop to meaner thoughts.'

and to secure freedom and religious liberty. If this be so, this also is part of the clergyman's work as Minister of the Word.

IV

Prior to the two great divisions of the clergyman's work which we have considered lies the obligation to study. His calling is one of the learned professions. He must always be a learner, and his life must be that of a student. Great harm is done when an ignorant person speaks in public ; but it is not for directly practical purposes only, or because of results, but for its own sake that he must love learning, because he believes in the power of truth. He must read, therefore, quite apart from doing what is necessary for the preparation of sermons, and must accustom himself to regard this as a definite part of his work to be done in his study. Things advertised as novelties in shops, and produced in factories, really originate in the minds of designers. In battle the council of war and plan of campaign demand higher qualities than the management of the commissariat or the ammunition of the fighting line ; so the hard work of thought is both mission work and service to the Church. Without science it is impossible to regard mere professional activity as satisfactory, nor, in a time of growing complication of social life and the accompanying elaboration of other callings, will the clergyman's work, if

The clergyman as a student.

science be lacking, be more than personal and individual. Study is necessary to see how the Church extended her borders in the past, how ideas can be spread to-day, to notice how society is changing, how customs originate. Instead of ignoring the experience of others, of clinging to antiquated methods, of nagging at 'indifference', or relying on talk, the clergy as experimental students need to formulate their policy, to abandon, it may be, the crude method of frontal attack, to forestall changes of opinion, and by getting at the springs of thought to influence it at its source.[1]

What the clergyman is not: (1) the professionally good man.
Such, then, may be said to be the work of an English clergyman. It remains briefly to say what it is not.

It is not that of the professional good man who

[1] R. W. Church, *Human Life and its Conditions*. 'The Twofold Debt of the Clergy' (Macmillan.) p. 165 : 'A clergyman ought to be a student—a reader and a thinker—to the very end. "I am still learning," said the greatest of artists in his old age of fame ("Ancora imparo," Michael Angelo). Nor, if there is the will, the habit of self-command, is that incompatible with a very busy ministry. At least, his own great subject he should seek to know, in the way that other things are known now by those who care for them.' The whole sermon may be read for a presentation of this side of the English conception of a clergyman. Cp. *The Book of Common Prayer*, 'The form and manner of Ordering of Priests': '*The Bishop*. Will you be diligent in Prayers, and in reading of the Holy Scriptures, and in such studies as help to the knowledge of the same, laying aside the study of the world and the flesh? *Answer*. I will endeavour myself so to do, the Lord being my helper.'

is 'paid for doing what is right'. He may chance
to be the head of society in the place where he
lives and, as the most conspicuous figure in it,
be bound to set an example, but, if so, this is
in virtue of his accidental position, not of his
calling. In this case his duty is exactly the same
as that of a layman in a similar position. Therefore, though to call on people may be a social duty,
it is no part of his professional work and should
not be suffered to interfere with it. If he is rich
it may be his duty to entertain, but as a clergyman he is under no obligation to invite 'his'
church workers to tea, to subscribe to football
clubs, or to head subscription lists. That there
are grave dangers to religion when a church has
a class ministry, or when its ministers are popularly associated with direct giving of relief, is
obvious to any one who regards the present
position of the English Church.[1]

Nor is the clergyman a mere moral policeman. (2) a moral policeman.
It may be useful for him to take the chair at smok-
ing concerts and so to prevent indecency, or to
spend evening after evening playing bagatelle or
keeping order in boys' clubs ; or, on the other hand,
these may be singularly expensive and ineffective
ways of doing what ought to be unnecessary
in the one case, and in the other could be done
better by an uneducated drill-sergeant, but in any

[1] I have dwelt more at length on this danger in my *Circumstances or Character ?* Part III, ' Religion and Relief.'

case it is not his work. These two false ideas
need seriously to be combated, as they obscure
the true conception of his duty, exhaust the energy
of our clergy, encourage laymen to acquiesce in
a lower standard of morality, create a clerical
caste, and deter men from seeking Holy Orders.

V

The
Pastoral
ideal.

To sum up, a clergyman, according to the
English ideal, works in four capacities : as a
student, as a manager, as a governor, and as
a missionary, it is his office to help his fellow men
in things spiritual. His calling runs parallel with
secular callings, often dealing with the same
material, but always with the distinction that
where others render mutual service in outward
things, he is concerned with the inner spiritual
life sacramentally mediated by them.   The
methods may be the same and the standard of
efficiency must be no lower, but the inspiration
and outlook is quite another.

A
student.

He must be a student. As a student of books
it is his duty to further the cause of theological
learning ; by original work, if he can, and, if he
cannot, by studying the works of others for the
purpose of teaching and making the results of
research available for the masses. But he must
also be a student of human documents, learning
to discern the needs of men and to read their

characters, observing the phenomena of spiritual life, testing them and experimenting as far as can be done with reverence for the souls of his fellow creatures. He must be a student of the laws and the eternal truths of religious life as revealed in history and as manifesting themselves in the world. He must believe in knowledge as of prior value to bodily activity. He must train himself to penetrate directly to the moral and spiritual issues in all he sees around him. As a musician educates his ear he must learn to sharpen his perceptions of right and wrong, or of religious import, in current literature, in the doings of society, in accepted customs of business, in social policy, so that he may be able to judge and interpret them to his fellow men. He must discipline his inner life to this end.

He is also a manager in an institution, that is, an administrator of things immediately under his hand in a particular part of the Church. This side of his work is practical, direct, and detailed. In the parish he has duties in a limited area and to a definite number of men. He has to deal with individual souls as the general practitioner deals with their bodies. The religious life of the parish centres in the church, and he has, with others, the care of the material things necessary for corporate expression of religious life, the guardianship of church buildings and furniture. He is responsible for the organization of public worship,

A manager.

and has to see that nothing becomes a hindrance to the reality of devotion. Like the manager of a business, like a director of a museum, library, school, or institution, he often has to look after things rather than to do them ; but as they, by so doing, help the flow of commerce, open the way to knowledge, or make available social benefits, so he attends to details to make straight the way to the people for corporate and individual access to Grace. He is the servant or minister to the Christian people, and as such is charged with its official representation, conducting its worship, the mouthpiece of its corporate prayer, keeping up the round of its formal worship day by day, maintaining the environment in which by God's grace religion thrives, charged with the ministry of the Word and Sacraments.

A governor.

As a governor in a polity his work is wider. He is not merely the minister of the congregation, but in the Orders of the whole Church. He therefore has to deal with larger matters not under his immediate supervision. Like a civil servant who works from an office, he is charged with his part of the government of the whole body. He is an official of a corporate institution, bound to consider the welfare of the whole and the interaction of its parts. In the parish he must act with a definite theory of government. He must do his own work in such a way that it may co-operate with that of his fellow clergymen in other parishes. He must do everything constitutionally on a thought-out conception of his calling, considering always the larger issues at stake. So far as its nature as scientific is concerned, this conception need not be sacerdotal or unsacerdotal, but it must be based on a reasoned theory, and be intelligible and explicable. In the diocese he must take his share in combined action, preserving his proportion of parochial and general interests. Here he is dealing with matters which, since their results cannot be directly traced, need for their handling the special gifts of government.

Finally, he is a missionary. This aspect of his work is not in danger of being lost sight of while preaching forms so large a part of his duties. But it need not be limited to this single method. Writing, distribution of literature, ' practical work ', above all, conscientious discharge of ordinary duties, are various ways of extending the influence of the Church. But all such work of propaganda must be undertaken after strict examination of its real effectiveness, and he must be always ready to drop methods that are proved useless, and to originate new plans which experience or analogy suggest as likely to succeed. A missionary.

One or other of these elements may predominate in the work of any individual. Indeed, specialization, either in study, in parish work, in diocesan service, or in missionary activity, is necessary for effective pioneer service ; but the specialist should bear in mind that his labour is but one element which he offers to the common catholic cause, and that his deficiency is made up in the Communion of Saints by that which every joint supplieth. And the creation of a scientific school of Pastoral Theology is needed in which to study each department separately and in its relation to the whole, so that a body of students may be trained in it for their future work.

CHAPTER II

THE TRAINING OF THE STUDENT

How is the agent in Pastoral Theology to be trained? We have considered why, for practical purposes, we shall do best if we take the clergyman as the type of all workers in the field, and our reasons for confining ourselves to the clergyman of the English Church. What, then, is the best way of training our clergy so that they may be such as will build up a school of Pastoral Theology of the kind that we desire? The training of the agent.

I

At the outset we are confronted by two obstacles, the almost universal disbelief in training of any sort that seems to be inherent in the English character, and a certain distrust of the current methods felt by those who recognize the necessity for training of some kind. The first of these need not detain us. We are all familiar with the general disbelief in education which leads the mass of working men to remove their children from school the moment the law allows them to do so, the widespread distrust of book-learning common to all classes, and the general resentment felt at the demand for clear thought which Disbelief in education.

'regards order as another form of tyranny'.[1]
We are not surprised, therefore, to see it reappear
when the training of the clergy is under discussion,
or to find it seek support from religious prejudice,
and nerve itself to opposition by the use of the
alliteration which ensures the success of party
cries, in attacking the 'seminary system'. The
same instinct that leads the artisan to remove
his boy from school because he 'thinks it is time
he began to learn something', can safely be
worked on to call out applause for a declaration
that it is better for the future clergyman to knock
about the world, or to go to Oxford House or to
Toynbee Hall, than to study the special duties
of his profession. No doubt such a knowledge of
the world and of men as can be gained in Settle-
ments is of great value as an addition to professional knowledge, but no one would suggest
it to a doctor as an alternative to study at a
hospital, nor ought it to be proposed as a substitute
for professional training for a clergyman. The
false idea that amateur work is superior to skilled

---

[1] *Life and Letters of Mandell Creighton*, by his wife (Longmans, 1906), vol. ii, p. 326 : ' Everything one gets is ultimately
dealt with in the terms of ordered thought, which gives a sense
of relationship between one impression and another, and an
end which keeps them all together. . . . There must be a scheme
of things somewhere if we are to have any impressions at all,
we cannot have minds like lumber rooms. There must be
some order. Yet the modern mind regards order as another
form of tyranny.'

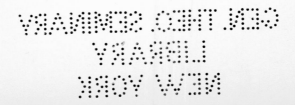

has been successfully fought in the professions of medicine and teaching, and with it have gone Mrs. Gamp and Mr. Squeers; it is being banished in the army and in the labour world, where it has brought about such disastrous results, and in the case of the clerical calling is being so vigorously attacked as to need little regard.

A more serious objection is that which is due to a certain distrust of our current methods of training, and those who are engaged in the work would be the first to confess that those methods are largely tentative and experimental. They would acknowledge that it is necessary to consider criticisms on them and to discover, if possible, their root defects. These criticisms generally take the form of accusations that the course is narrowing, that it is unpractical, and that it is inadequate. *Criticisms of current methods of training.*

An accusation of narrowness is easily made but is difficult to prove or to disprove, and as a criticism is generally too vague to be helpful. Sometimes it merely means that the critic is of a different school of thought from that of the institution he criticizes. But till we have found a philosophy which shall reconcile all opposing antitheses we cannot regard as narrow every view from which some one else differs. It may be observed that this accusation is generally made by persons who have no knowledge from within of the working of the system that they condemn, and, as a matter of fact, the experience of those who have been at *As narrowing.*

Theological Colleges seems to point the other way. It is true, perhaps, that many of the students who leave them are still insufficiently educated, but, as has been pointed out, it is not quite fair to condemn a Theological College for failing to do in one year what a University has not previously succeeded in doing in three.

As un-practi-cal.

The accusation of unpracticalness is less easily met. No doubt the training is too academic, and the relevancy of its studies to the duties of after-life is not made sufficiently clear. A student who looks forward to ' work among boys ' finds it difficult to see how the study of Hebrew, and of the proofs of the Thirty-Nine Articles, is fitting him for his task. This robs studies of their interest, and leaves practical work unintelligent in after-life.

As in-ade-quate.

To the accusation of inadequacy no defence is made. It is acknowledged that one year after a University course, or two years at a non-graduate Theological College after a broken educa-tion, can only give a training that is ridiculously insufficient.

To find the remedy for these defects it is neces-sary to get clear the different factors of the problem. When these are disentangled it will be found that in each case greater efficiency will remove the objection made. To escape narrow-ness we need a clear conception of scientific method ; this is a question of general education.

To preserve the teaching from irrelevancy and to get the just proportions of academic and practical work, we need a clear conception of the natures of Theology and of Pastoral Theology and of the relation of the one to the other. To make the preparation adequate we must have a living science of Pastoral Theology in which to train the student. The first two needs have been already considered, and for the third we have seen that the school has yet to be created and that before this can be done the agent, that is the clergyman, must be trained.

II

Ideally the places in which these three questions should be dealt with are the school for education, the University for the science, and the parish for practical training. While the method adopted in each stage would be based on that which had gone before, the lessons learned would be carried on into that which was to follow. Education begun at the school would be continued at the University and all through life ; the theological view of the world gained by prolonged study would direct practical experience. Unfortunately, the machinery for scientific practical training does not exist in the parish, so that the abstract science has not been built up and cannot therefore be studied or taught adequately

The place of training.

at the University. The only course that is open is, therefore, to go right back to the beginning, to recognize that at present we cannot really train the agent, that we must go back a step farther and consider the training of the student who in time will become the agent, and, later on, himself the trainer.

The Theo-logical College.

In considering the training of the student it will be assumed that he will be trained in a Theological College either at a University town or elsewhere. Apart from the obvious practical advantages it affords for organized teaching, common life has an educational value in itself. This is recognized in our University system for men, whatever may be said for or against the boarding-school system for boys. But in the case of the clergy this advantage becomes almost a necessity, since the students are seeking to qualify for positions in a corporate body, in which, as an Order, they will have to work together, and the power of co-operation is a thing that has to be learned. Moreover, they will form a body separated from the laity, and if they are to mix freely with them, they must be so familiar with their position that they are not self-conscious in it. It is only if they are at home in their peculiar state of life that they will feel no need of self-assertion or apology, and this naturalness can most easily and naturally be acquired by the corporate life of a special college.

But when we come to consider the form such a college course should take, the inherent difficulties of the problem are increased. The practical needs of the Church exert a constant pressure on students to cut down the time of their preparation. The shortage in the supply of candidates for Orders tempts the authorities to accept inferior men, and hampers them in rejecting the less fit. The fear of missing present opportunities in parish work would lead many incumbents to offer a steady resistance to any thorough scheme of training after ordination to the diaconate. Moreover, the variety and independence of the already existing institutions for training candidates, while valuable as leaving scope for experiments and initiative, makes it difficult to select or frame ideal conditions, or to say what is practicable at the present time.

But, leaving out the question of practical training for the present, we see that, whichever scheme is adopted, at least two elements must be kept in view, namely, the necessity of education and that of specialist work. The teaching must be of the University type and standard, and the relationship of Theology to Pastoral Theology must be kept steadily in view. Whether the teaching is at the University, whether it is given at a special Theological College after a degree has been taken, or whether the whole is given elsewhere by University-trained teachers, the best

General education and special training.

students only, perhaps, being sent to the University, the whole must be in touch with the centres of learning to keep it from becoming unscientific and empirical. And whether the pastoral element is only present in the mind of the lecturer, provided by special lecturers in a distinct Faculty, secured by personal influences, or guaranteed by special colleges or hostels at the Universities, or by Theological Colleges elsewhere, the need of both Theology and Pastoral Theology must be continuously and clearly borne in mind.

Two me- thods.

Keeping these two points before us, we shall see that the main differences in the various existing systems lie in the relations of the one study to the other and in the times and places where each is pursued. Either the student should first be given the best general education possible and then be made to turn his trained faculties to the study of Theology and Pastoral Theology, or his mind should be trained by the best theological education possible and he should then turn his trained faculties to the study of the world. If the first be considered the better plan, the ideal preparation would be an Arts course completed by postgraduate study in Theology both undertaken at the University, followed by a year's training in Pastoral Theology at a Theological College ; if the second, it would be a purely theological course at the University or elsewhere, followed by, or running concurrently with, special study of Pastoral Theology.[1]

There is yet a further difficulty connected with the subject-matter in which the student is to be Lack of suitable subject-matter.

---

[1] The most complete and fully carried out examples of the two systems may be found in England in the courses at the College of the Resurrection at Mirfield and Leeds and at the House of the Sacred Mission at Kelham. The post-graduate courses of the Theological Colleges at Cuddesdon, Wells, Ely, Leeds, Liverpool, Ripon, Llandaff, Newcastle, Farnham, Wycliffe Hall, Oxford, Ridley Hall and the Clergy Training School, Cambridge, and Trinity College, Dublin, are based on the first conception, though many of them have students who have already studied Theology at the University. The courses at King's College, London, St. David's, Lampeter, St. John's Hall, Highbury, St. Aidan's, Birkenhead, St. Paul's, Burgh, Bishop's Court, Isle of Man, and at the Colleges at Chichester, Lichfield, Salisbury, Warminster, Lincoln, Dorchester, Durham, and Manchester, are based on the second, though many of them receive students who have already taken a degree in subjects other than Theology at a University and shorten their theological course on that ground. (The training of the clergy of the Church of Rome, of the State Churches of Protestant Germany, and of the English Nonconformists generally, though widely differing in method, are based on the second conception.)

For details of these courses see the *Handbook of the Theological Colleges of the Church of England*, published annually by Messrs. Longmans, 39 Paternoster Row, London, E.C., and the appendices of the *Report of the Archbishop of Canterbury's Committee on the Supply and Training of Candidates for Holy Orders*, June 1908.

For a further discussion of the whole question see *England and the Church* (Longmans, 1902), and a supplement *The Church and the Ordination Question* (The S.S.M. Press, Kelham, Newark-upon-Trent, 1907), by the Rev. H. Kelly, Director of the Society of the Sacred Mission.

trained. Just as the field of the parish lacks the proper machinery for training the agent, so the mental field of the college is largely that of pure Theology and lacks the peculiar material for the special training of the student. This, in our present state of knowledge is inevitable, and the main part of his studies must remain purely theological. But it should be his aim, an aim in which his tutors should help him, continually to 'pastoralize' (if we may coin the word) all that he learns—to study it, that is, directly in view of its practical application, or at least to direct his attention to that side of his work from time to time. Under the former of the two above-mentioned schemes, where the student has already studied his Theology, the whole course would be pastoral ; the scientific method already learned at the University would be applied now to Theology in its personal application in the service of his fellow men. In the present state of the science this would mainly consist of the study of Homiletics, a subject which has been well worked at, and of Liturgics and the Prayer Book, in which much remains still to be done. In the second type of college the teaching would be mainly theological until it may become possible for pastoral teaching to be given side by side with it.

The aim of the College. We have, then, to consider the problem of training the student of Pastoral Theology in a Theo-

logical College ; the aim that we need to keep
before us is that of forming in him the right type
of mind that later on will produce a scientific
worker.   Just as the *Magistri Comacini*[1] evolved an
art by creating a school of artists—an experiment
that has been attempted again in our own day
in the mosaic work in St. Paul's Cathedral—so to
create the science of Pastoral Theology must we
begin by training a body of students.   The Theological College may also have for its aim instruction
in Theology, and under present conditions, at any
rate, this is a necessity, but in what follows this
side will only be alluded to.   The main purpose
that we have to consider is the production of the
peculiar scientific temper which, as we saw, is
most difficult to acquire as well as most fruitful
in results when exercised in the study of the
highest things.

Again, it must be made clear that the purpose
of a Theological College is not to ' teach a man
his work '.   That a practical apprenticeship is
necessary has long been recognized, but no art can
be properly taught before it is studied.   The
necessary training can only be given effectively
in the parish, a thing impossible at present, and
will always be of little use by itself without
science, except, maybe, for a class of inferior

(marginal note:) Not to ' teach a man his work '.

---

[1] Cp. F. X. Kraus, *Geschichte der christlichen Kunst*, Bd. I,
s. 598, who refers to Muratori, *Antiq. Diss.*, t. xxiv.   Cp. also
J. Burckhardt, *Der Cicerone*, Achte Auflage, 1901, p. 25.

lay workers who are only intended to work mechanically as sergeants under the higher officers of the Church, and are content to obey without fully understanding the reasons of their orders.

Therefore in the college all outside 'practical work' should be resolutely checked. Its only value lies in its keeping the student in touch with reality, and this can equally well be secured by work carried on under supervision and with criticism as part of the mental training of the course, such as teaching in schools and visiting under direction from a Charity Organization office, or, where this is not practicable because of the shortness of the course, by visits paid to schools and institutions. Work done by the light of nature, nominally to 'get experience' but more often with the desire to help rather than to learn, only stereotypes the student in bad or traditional methods; it distracts him from his proper studies, since the human beings that he deals with are certain to interest him more than books. Moreover, it seems strangely presumptuous to do what no one in any other profession would dare to do. No doctor would begin to practise before he was qualified, and it betrays a very low conception of religious work to think that for it any amateur effort will do. Short-handed vicars should not be allowed to exploit students to their future detriment any more than manufacturers should be suffered to build up their trade on boy labour.[1]

Again, it must be made clear that a college is not a place intended merely to prepare men for examinations. But it is not of much use to repeat this so long as admission to Holy Orders is made to depend on the results of answers given to set papers. Till the present custom is abolished, and a wider interpretation given to the guarantee of the archdeacon as to the fitness of candidates, it is almost impossible to make the work at a Theological College really satisfactory. The ordination examination is bound to influence the whole course of study, and is no real test even of intellectual efficiency. It is not fair to reject a man after two or three years of preparation, and practically it is not done. The candidate who fails is merely put off, and after another six months' desultory reading, generally done in the interval of 'lay work', often living in very straitened circumstances or forced to run into debt, is no more fitted for ordination than he was before. For this examination might well be substituted a paper at the beginning of his training to test his intellectual

Nor 'to prepare for examination'.

[1] Certain colleges lay great stress on practical work. My experience from inside was that, except for the slight value of a certain sense of being in touch with real things that it gave—a result that could easily have been secured in other ways—the visiting we did was worse than useless. Since then I have seen incalculable harm done by men spoiling their time of preparation by 'practical work'.

capacity, but personal references (the givers of which should be seen) are far more valuable even for this purpose. Then, after the candidate has been seen and provisionally accepted, the reports of his tutors should be relied upon. If, in the opinion of those who are watching him, a candidate is not ready—and some men develop more slowly than others—his time of probation should be extended, and financial help should be forthcoming for such extra time of study so that no one should be allowed to enter the diaconate before he was fit. Only under some such plan will it become possible adequately to train the student of Pastoral Theology.

The particular courses of study vary, and must vary, in different colleges, but this does not affect the matter we are considering. It is not necessary for our purpose to examine the contents of each syllabus, as the training of the mind is practically independent of the particular departments of theological study over which it is exercised. It has been remarked that though there are many books on teaching, it is curious to note how few there are on learning. This is perhaps natural when we remember that most teaching is given to children to whom it is neither easy nor desirable always to explain processes, but it is good for elder students to be conscious of the purpose of their tutors. In what follows the emphasis will be laid upon teaching, but it must be remembered that after all the success of the tutor depends in great measure on the co-operation of the student, and that the training in a Theological College must itself be largely self-training.[1]

III

Our aim is, therefore, to see how the work done can be made to serve as a training in scientific method. For this we must follow the steps marked out above in Book I, ch. i, and consider how it can be made to educate the student in concentration, in observation, in criticism, in synthesis, in exposition, in deduction, and in imagination. This is to be done at present more by theological matter than by pastoral subjects. The former usually consists of languages and exegesis, dogmatic Theology, Church History, Philosophy, and Essay Writing, while Pastoral Theology is generally confined to Homiletics and study of the Prayer Book, with a certain amount of instruction in rhetoric and elocution, and isolated lectures in educational, social, and parochial matters. It is not necessary to consider these from the point of view of their theological contents, or to discuss what subjects or books should be selected ; we are for our purpose only

The aim to train in scientific method.

[1] For an example of a work written to guide the learner the student may be referred to Fr. H. Kelly's admirable little books, *The Aims and Methods of Theological Study* and *The Continuation of Study*, published by the Society of the Sacred Mission, Kelham, Newark-upon-Trent.

concerned with the question, ' What needs special emphasis in the method by which they are studied, and how can they be made to train the student's mental faculties in the peculiar way required ? '

The course limited to Theology.

First of all we see that we are justified in limiting the subjects of study to these purely theological matters.   It is the first condition of scientific work that we should define our subject, and concentrate our attention on it.   This needs to be emphasized since the authorities are constantly urged to assimilate the courses in Theological Colleges to Arts courses by the introduction of non-theological subjects, a request prompted by a general disbelief in the existence, or at least the value, of Theology as a science.

The justification of this limitation lies in the fact that our aim is to give the student a peculiar cast of mind, as is done for other professions, so that he may learn to recognize the particular aspect of things on which he is to qualify himself to speak. The result will be that his outlook will be at once broader and less superficial ; he will not be distracted, during his training, by a number of conflicting interests which he can only know on the surface, but will learn to see the whole of one subject as far as his mind can grasp it and to realize how its parts stretch out indefinitely in all directions.   The conditions under which he is living in the college are confessedly artificial and abnormal, but they are temporary, and have for

their object the securing of that thoroughness and
efficiency which will enable him, later on, to mix
with other thorough and efficient craftsmen, and
so to be able to appreciate their points of view.

The basis of scientific method is, as we saw, The
laid by accurate observation and recording. Stress $\frac{habit}{}$ of ob-
should therefore be laid on the habit of note- serva-
taking. The tutor should at the beginning of his $\frac{tion~and}{record}$-
training look over the student's notes, or at least ing.
discuss the matter with him to be sure that he has
the habit of taking them and sees its purpose.
This, it should be realized, is not to help him
remember what is noted, though a thing written
is more easily recalled;[1] nor is it primarily of value
to store facts for future reference ; its *first* purpose
is to teach the student to see clearly what is
peculiar or characteristic in anything he comes
across. Notes should at first be taken of everything, even of subjects which may already be
known well, simply to acquire the habit of attention and observation. This can be done over the
ordinary work of lectures. Training in accuracy
will be ensured by the habit of putting down dates,
and by experiencing the waste of time caused by
insufficient or careless noting of references. Exercise in penetration will be involved in the continual attempt to put down in few words (not in
shorthand) the gist of what the lecturer says,

[1] The tutor will probably find that many students at first
make summaries of their lectures, which are easy to visualize
with the object of reproducing them in examinations.

while at the same time width of observation, and sensitiveness to literary and logical structure, will be got by analysing books and ' displaying ' (to borrow a term from printers) their contents in outlines.   And, generally, the aim of the student will be to gain a taste for reading and to accustom himself to hear and see things.

Of this faculty of observation the habit of recording is an essential element.   The student should be warned against the fallacy of trying to ' strengthen his memory ', and should be led to see how understanding the relations of things is the best way to have them at command when we want to recall them, while a substitute for mechanical memorizing can be found in mechanical method.[1] He should learn to put everything on paper, and every isolated note on a separate piece of paper. He should accustom himself to systematic keeping of tablet, note, and commonplace, books.   This power of observation can be stimulated by making students write essays describing things they have noticed in different parishes or elsewhere, as Flaubert taught his pupils to use their eyes,[1] or

[1] Guy de Maupassant, *Pierre et Jean* (Paris, 1902), Introduction, *Le Roman*, p. xxx.   After saying how he came to know Flaubert and to profit by his advice, the author writes : ' La moindre chose contient un peu d'inconnu.   Trouvons-le. Pour décrire un feu qui flambe et un arbre dans une plaine, demeurons en face de ce feu et de cet arbre jusqu'à ce qu'ils ne ressemblent plus, pour nous, à aucun autre arbre et à aucun autre feu.   C'est de cette façon qu'on devient original.

' Quand vous passez, me disait-il, devant un épicier assis

by their taking part in organized charitable work in which they will have to write accurate reports on case papers of visits paid by them to various persons.[1]   By the end of his period of training the habit of observation and of recording what he has seen will have become part of the nature of the student.

sur sa porte, devant un concierge qui fume sa pipe, devant une station de fiacres, montrez-moi cet épicier, et ce concierge, leur pose, toute leur apparence physique contenant aussi, indiquée par l'adresse de l'image, toute leur nature morale, de façon à ce que je ne les confonde avec aucun autre épicier, ou avec aucun autre concierge, et faites-moi voir, par un seul mot, en quoi un cheval de fiacre ne ressemble pas aux cinquante autres qui le suivent et le précèdent.'   (In the smallest thing there is something we do not know.   Let us find it out.   If we want to describe a fire alight or a tree in the open, we must stay before this fire or this tree till, for us, it is no longer like any other tree or any other fire.   This is how we write things that are our own.

He used to say ' when you pass by a man sitting at the door of his little general shop, a concierge smoking his pipe, or a cab-stand, show me this general dealer and this concierge, their attitude, their whole external appearance, and with it, by the art of your picture, their whole inner character, so that I shall not mistake them for any other general dealer or concierge, and make me see by a single word wherein a cab-horse is unlike the fifty others seen before or after it.)

Cp. Browning, *Fra Lippo Lippi* :

> Have you noticed, now,
> Your cullion's hanging face ?   A bit of chalk
> And trust me but you should, though !   How much more
> If I drew higher things with the same truth !

[1] Cp. my *Charitable Relief*, Handbooks for the Clergy Series (Longmans), 2nd ed., 1908, ch. ii.

The critical faculty.

But mere sharpness of vision is valueless in itself, and to record everything observed is a mere useless labour ; there must therefore be in the student the critical spirit which will discriminate between that which has importance and that which may be disregarded. The mere fact of noticing a thing involves some initial criticism ; in the use made of observation there is much more that is still unconscious ; but the critical faculty can be stimulated and trained, and brought into conscious and regulated activity.

This can also be done in the ordinary course of lectures. The student of textual and higher criticism will find an interest in his work apart from the understanding it gives him of the meaning of the Bible, when he realizes that he is being taught to notice the importance of minute differences in its words, and to exercise his judgement on personal and psychological phenomena revealed in the phrases of its several authors. In studying the reasons for believing in the authenticity and genuineness of the Fourth Gospel, or in the Resurrection of Our Lord, he is not only establishing his conviction that he is reading a first-hand authority, or that his hope is not vain, but is incidentally learning the laws of evidence by tracing out converging and complicated threads of proof. In reading the history of the Christological controversies of the fourth and fifth centuries he is exercising himself in criticism of terms as he experiences the difficulties of exact theological expression, and in his rigorous examination of ancient heresies, or in ' verifying the quotations ' of their modern counterparts he is being taught criticism of accuracy.

The first stages of the application of such methods in Pastoral Theology can also be taken in hand even in the present imperfect state of the science. The study of Phonetics will not merely make the student notice, and avoid, actual errors in pronunciation, but, by training his ear, will make him critical and sensitive to the slight varieties of expression and intonation which give to careful speech its special charm. In the study of the Prayer Book he will learn judgement of taste as he familiarizes himself with the dignity of its liturgical structure and the majesty of its language. In endeavouring to form his style by writing and in practising the art of delivery, the same education of critical taste can be secured, while in Homiletics, by drawing up outlines of sermons and discussing their contents by the Socratic method of dialectic, criticism of worth can be exercised. In the whole social life of the college the student has opportunities of learning judgement of character, of getting to recognize the signs which show when a man knows what he is talking about. In his reading he may get the faculty of picking out those books which bear the mark of truth, not merely by familiarity with the names of those who are referred to again and again as having credit among scholars, but because, like the men of Samaria, he can hear for himself when a thing is said with authority.

Concen-
tration
of at-
tention.
But even when gathered with the natural selection of a critical mind, observations crowd on one another and notes accumulate. The student must, therefore, learn to concentrate his attention, and to sustain his inquiries along selected lines of thought. This is specially necessary under the complicated conditions of modern life where so many distractions and varied interests call off attention in all directions. If he is not to fritter away his energies, if he is to acquire lucidity, relevancy, and thoroughness, he must learn to direct his energies to a point.

This is done by lectures from the fact that they are given in courses. The small use of a single lecture is soon realized. The mental training involved, say, in spending a whole term in setting out in order the arguments for Theism, with an adequate consideration of the modifications made in them by changes in philosophical thought, and of the practical use to which they can be put in apologetic, and of side issues such as the problem of pain, is of far more value than the actual acquisition of ' proofs ' which do not convince.[1]

[1] Cp. Pascal, *Pensées*, ed. Brunschvicg, No. 543 : ' Les preuves de Dieu métaphysiques sont si éloignées du raisonnement des hommes, et si impliquées, qu'elles frappent peu ;

Or again, the value of a study of the Reformation Period lies not merely in the fact that the opposing parties reappear in different guise to-day in society, in the religious world, and in each individual in varying proportions, but perhaps even more in the mental exercise it gives in sustained examination of conflicting schools of thought, and in the grouping of facts on either side.

The setting of special books to read is sometimes deprecated as likely to hinder initiative and the power of independent observation, but at least it compels the student to concentrate his attention on big books and standard works—on books that make him think—and to turn away from little controversial manuals. He will not then need to consider the mass of little lesser apologetic works that are issued, while the superficial attacks on Christianity, which these are designed to meet, he will find easy to deal with after the study of first-class works by the impetus acquired in the greater effort.[1]   The same end

et quand cela servirait à quelques-uns, cela ne servirait que pendant l'instant qu'ils voient cette démonstration, mais une heure après ils craignent de s'être trompés.' (The metaphysical proofs of God are so remote from the reasoning of men, and so complicated, that they make little impression ; and if they should be of service to some, it would be only during the moment that they see such demonstration ; but an hour afterwards they fear they have been mistaken.) Cp also No. 556.

[1] The feeling of ease in doing a lesser work after a great effort is a fact of common experience, and care should be taken that every student has had this experience and been conscious of it.

can be aimed at in writing essays. While at an earlier stage they may be merely descriptive and set to stimulate observation, later on subjects may be given which require more selection and arrangement. These must almost necessarily be connected with work being done in the regular course, as a student will hardly have enough time for independent research, or original thought on other subjects, to make them of any value to him. Sermons may similarly be written which use the material of lectures, not as sermons to be preached but simply as exercises in the practical application of studies and in selection of points relevant to a special single end.

Understanding and knowledge.
In all this the aim should be to make the student understand the laws of learning, not merely as a part of the abstract study of Psychology but experimentally in himself. He should learn to recognize when he knows a thing ; [1] he should have experienced the mental trouble and indecision that precedes the bringing of a matter to birth as his own mental offspring ; [2] he should be

[1] R. W. Church, *Human Life and its Conditions*, p. 166 : ' The men who influence the thoughts of their time are not those who try to know all things, but those who have learned one thing so well that they know, and show to others also, *what knowing means.*'

[2] An illustration of the contrast of a thing struggled with and a thing mastered may be found in I Cor. viii. 7, where St. Paul is grappling with the immediate problem whether Christians may eat meat offered to idols, and Rom. xiv., where he has thought out the whole question and has settled it on fundamental principles.

familiar with the unmistakable feeling that we
experience when, after soaking in a subject for
some time, we find we have absorbed all we want of
it and can at last express it coloured by our personality with lucidity and easy mastery. The difference between understanding possessed as soon as
a subject presents no difficulties, and knowledge
only to be claimed when it has been grasped and
can be reproduced, can be tested by examinations. These should, therefore, be frequent, and
a great responsibility rests on the examiner to
make them serve this end; but it must be clearly
understood that the final acceptance for Holy
Orders does not depend on them but on something
very different, or they will defeat their own purpose and become mere inducements to cramming.

So far the discipline we have been considering
has been mainly that of subjection to the thought
of others, whether imposed by the tutor on the
mind of the student in lectures, or by voluntary
action on his own part in preparation of sermon
outlines and essays or in reading; even in simple
observation of facts he has to submit himself to
them and see them as they are. This reading and
writing makes a full and exact man; what is now
wanted is the conference which will make a ready
man. The student has now to learn to generalize
and make deductions, to find out the causes of
things, to originate ideas based on the sure
ground of wide, critical, and sustained observa-

*Gener-
aliza-
tion and
deduc-
tion.*

tion, to give to all the ideas he has made his own the peculiar personal touch that makes them valuable, to exercise his imagination now no longer a ' forward delusive faculty ever obtruding beyond its sphere ',[1] ' that mistress of error and falsity ',[2] but ' the free generation of thoughts whereby we come to a conception of the world ' :[3]

> another name for absolute power
> And clearest insight, amplitude of mind,
> And Reason in her most exalted mood.[4]

In the second stage (the second year in a two years' course) this element can be made to predominate. The tutor will aim at making his lectures less didactic and more suggestive. They will probably be fewer in number, and sermon and essay writing will occupy more of the student's time. But the chief factor in stimulating originality of thought will be the common life of the college. Irresponsible debates among the students do much to quicken fertility of mind, and are invaluable if they are not taken too seriously. On the other hand, to get outsiders to open discussions of ' subjects of the day ' is undesirable if it leads men to deliver opinions (as distinct from

[1] Butler, *Analogy*, Part I, ch. i.

[2] Pascal, *Pensées*, ed. Brunschvicg, No. 82. Cp. R. W. Church, *Pascal and other Sermons* (Macmillan, 1896), p. 318.

[3] Schleiermacher, quoted in *Selections from the Literature of Theism*, by A. Caldecott and H. R. Mackintosh (T. & T. Clark, Edinburgh, 1904), p. 299.

[4] Wordsworth, *The Prelude*, Book XIV.

asking questions) on matters which as students
they cannot possibly know sufficiently thoroughly
to form an opinion of any value on them.   But
it is ' not only in courts of law and other public
assemblies, but also in private conversation on
matters great and small ' that ' correct use of
language is held in equal honour whether the
subject to which it is applied is trivial or important '.[1]   Just as in practical work attendance
at committees is necessary, if for no other reason,
because from the companionship of fellow workers
enthusiasm becomes contagious, and we learn
again to believe in our cause, so common life is
almost a necessity for fertility of thought.   The
tutor can do something, and contact with a
first-class, original, or even merely a sincere and
older, mind is always of value, but it is what
one student does for another that really counts.
It is rather in close personal intercourse, in easy
talk round the fire on a winter's evening, in long
walks together, in eager discussions reaching far
into the night, when we held debate

> on mind and art,
> And labour, and the changing mart,
> And all the framework of the land,[2]

[1] Plato, *Phaedrus* 261, tr. J. Wright (Macmillan's ' Golden
Treasury' Series) Ἆρ' οὖν οὐ τὸ μὲν ὅλον ἡ ῥητορικὴ ἂν εἴη τέχνη
ψυχαγωγία τις διὰ λόγων, οὐ μόνον ἐν δικαστηρίοις καὶ ὅσοι ἄλλοι
δημόσιοι σύλλογοι, ἀλλὰ καὶ ἐν ἰδίοις, ἡ αὐτὴ σμικρῶν τε καὶ μεγάλων
πέρι; καὶ οὐδὲν ἐντιμότερον τό γε ὀρθὸν περὶ σπουδαῖα ἢ περὶ φαῦλα
γιγνόμενον;   [2] Cp. Tennyson, *In Memoriam*, lxxxvii.

that, we find when we have grown older, those beliefs were made clear that have stood by us through
life, and those convictions forged which we have
striven to express as our message to the world.
Later on wisdom comes differently ; she shows
herself in the patient pursuit of carefully planned
work, or in the course of reading on quiet mornings
when the mind follows the course of thought of
some master of literature or religion who ' soothes
distraction down ', and is set free to receive
inspirations and to see visions of things great and
true ; but whether in youth or maturity, it is
the worker who is trained and disciplined in
scientific method who always keeps the power to
see new truth.[1]

[1] Cp. W. Bagehot, *Literary Studies*, ' Oxford ', vol. iii,
pp. xiv and 101 (Longmans) : ' So, too, in youth, the real
plastic energy is not in tutors, or lectures, or in books "got up",
but in Wordsworth and Shelley, in the books that all read
because all like ; in what all talk of because all are interested ;
in the argumentative walk or disputatious lounge ; in the
impact of young thought upon young thought, of fresh
thought on fresh thought, of hot thought on hot thought ;
in mirth and refutation, in ridicule and laughter ; for these
are the free play of the natural mind, and these cannot be
got without a college.'

Cp. also Augustine, *Confessions*, Book IV, ch. viii : ' Col-
loqui et corridere, et vicissim benevole obsequi ; simul legere
libros dulciloquos, simul nugari, et simul honestari ; dissentire
interdum sine odio, tanquam ipse homo secum, atque ipsa
rarissima dissensione condire consensiones plurimas ; docere
aliquid invicem, aut discere ab invicem ; desiderare absentes
cum molestia, suscipere venientes cum laetitia : his atque

When the right to speak and act has thus been Exposi-
earned the art of expression may be studied. The tion.
student has next to learn the machinery of exposition, all that in literature and speech, to which
the college course is mainly confined, is known as
style and rhetoric.

Therefore some lectures, at least, should be given
as models of form to set a standard of lucid and
balanced exposition. Practice in elocution should
be insisted on, not merely because exactness and
ease of language react on thought and make it
accurate and full, but also because it is an art that
provides an instrument to make explicit the ideas
within. The object being to train the powers of
expression, and not one immediately utilitarian,
practice should be found in reading and declaiming
passages of general literature, and not of the
Church services. The study of music has its place

huiusmodi signis a corde amantium et redamantium proce-
dentibus per os, per linguam, per oculos, et mille motus
gratissimos, quasi fomitibus conflare animos, et ex pluribus
unum facere.' (The talk, the laughter, the courteous mutual
deference, the common study of the masters of eloquence, the
comradeship now grave, now gay, the differences that left no
sting, as of a man differing with himself, the spice of disagree-
ment which seasoned the monotony of consent. Each by
turns would instruct or listen ; the absent were always missed,
the present always welcome. Such tokens springing from the
hearts of mutual friends, and displayed by a word, a glance,
an expression, by a thousand pretty complaisances, supply the
heat which welds souls together, and makes one of many.
Tr. C. Bigg, Methuen's ' Library of Devotion '.)

here because melody is called in to express in Christian worship things that lie too deep for words. The different conditions of public and private speech should be studied experimentally. The privileges of the platform, where we may say things naturally about which at ordinary times we are silent, the justification of the apparent contrast of ordinary conversation, in which we often talk superficially to protect ourselves and to conceal our thought, with preaching when we can say what we really believe, should have become matters that have been already considered before the student leaves the college. Otherwise he will later on have to face the difficult task of adjusting them for himself without guidance.

The delivery by the student of sermons for criticism, especially if before his fellow students, is of doubtful value. It is inevitably regarded as a mere exercise, and, if he regards it as something unreal, there can be no real criticism of expression. The giving of actual addresses in mission halls is of more worth, and may be useful when the student has reached a later stage of his training, but unless a competent critic is present, he may be only fixing himself in bad habits, while, if his tutor is there, it is hard for the preacher to forget his presence. All, or nearly all, the advantages sought by the practice could be obtained by the far more useful discipline of giving criticism lessons in a school before a trained teacher.

The feeling that comes when we have mas- Original
tered a subject may be unmistakable; ease and work.
facility in reproducing it may have been acquired;
but there is all the difference between mere
exposition and original work. Conviction is the
great prompter of eloquence; the man keen to
say a thing does not have to hunt for words.[1]
When the student has assimilated his knowledge
and made it his own, when he speaks no longer
with cocksureness but with authority, his training
is complete. But this comes only with experience
of life, *si vis me flere, dolendum est prius tibi*, and
the number of subjects on which he has earned

[1] Cp. Goethe, *Faust*:
 Wenn ihr's nicht fühlt, ihr werdet's nicht erjagen,
Wenn es nicht aus der Seele dringt
Und mit urkräftigem Behagen
Die Herzen aller Hörer zwingt.
. . . . . .
Doch werdet ihr nie Herz zu Herzen schaffen
Wenn es euch nicht von Herzen geht.

Und wenn's euch Ernst ist, was zu sagen,
Ist's nötig, Worten nachzujagen?

 (Yourself must feel it first, your end to capture,
Unless from out the soul it well,
And with a fresh resistless rapture
Your hearers' very hearts compel—
. . . . . .
But heart to heart ye will not sway and fashion
Save in your heart ye feel it first.

If ye've a message to deliver
Need ye for words be hunting ever?)
  (Tr. A. G. Latham, in Dent's 'Everyman's Library.')

the right to speak grows only by joy and suffering, by work and patience, as the years roll on.

This is the final goal of scientific study, but all has not yet been said. All that has been suggested above applies to any science if the subject-matter of study be changed. But in the higher sciences it is the creation of the right tone and temper that matters most, and in the highest, in Theology, in all its branches it is this which gives the student insight, and this therefore which is the chief aim of his time of preparation.

IV

The peculiar conditions of clerical life.

There are special difficulties peculiar to the training of a clergyman, and in the life of a Theological College. The conditions are confessedly unnatural, created for a special purpose, and established for a fixed time; the period of preparation is deliberately set apart for this work of specializing. But its aim is to make the after-life of the priest natural and normal, to fit him to live healthily in the environment in which his lot will be cast. He will have to be occupied with theological thought and teaching, and with administration of religious matters for many more hours than is the average man; his devotional life, therefore, must be correspondingly developed to keep the balance true. It is not by reaction, by secularizing his spare time, by pretending to be unclerical, by eccentricity, that he will make himself in his calling as the layman is in his, but by keeping the relation of his inner life to his handling of sacred things the same in proportion, though not in quantity as is fitting for every man.[1]

Moreover, the student is in after-life to be a servant of the community, and his inner life will not be entirely at his own disposal. He will have to speak of religious matters, and pray at stated times irrespectively of his inclinations or of his fluctuating sense of the reality of spiritual things. He needs, therefore, to have a great reserve of spiritual experience to draw upon, and a continuous round of habit to act as a flywheel to carry on its power. For this reason he must have a sufficiently long stay in a college to enable him to recast his whole religious life and to adapt it to new conditions. This adaptation must be a growth ; so he must live a common life with others where religion is openly and frankly recognized in all its outward expressions. Some of these he will possibly not keep up afterwards ; the precise form of observing fast-days which is natural in a community may not be suitable for domestic life ; others, such as the daily recitation in common of Matins and Evensong, should so become part of the routine of his existence that he will

Spiritual training.

---

[1] Clergymen are sometimes exercised by the fact that in their holidays they drop various religious practices. But this is surely natural and right. They are for the time, and for the special purpose of recreation, retiring to the position of laymen. Their professional duties are slackened and their inner life is correspondingly less intense.

never willingly omit to say his Offices as long as he lives, and will always feel that he and his fellow students are gathered together twice a day to make their common supplications. By constant attendance at the Eucharist he will come to feel at home at the altar, so that, later on, he will find that he has already learned to readjust himself to his new position in public worship—a change far greater than he had realized—and to be free from self-consciousness when called upon to celebrate. It will be by the regular habit of meditation, so hard to acquire except where it is the custom of a body of men, that his mind will be hallowed, rather than by continual addresses and exhortations, which, though valuable, are too like lectures and may easily leave the will passive and inert.[1]

If the student has once lived such a life he will always be able to go back to it in his mind. If his college was situated in picturesque surroundings, if he had the advantage of a beautiful chapel, if there was anything of that around which sentiment and affection naturally gather, so much the better, but at least he can retain the sense of corporate fellowship, of community of aim and purpose, and keep it alive by his intercessions for his fellow students ministering in God's kingdom or gathered together to prepare for His service.

[1] Cp. H. P. Liddon, *Clerical Life and Work*, ' The Priest in his Inner Life' (Longmans, 1894), originally published in *The Ecclesiastic and Theologian*, October 1856 and January 1857.

CHAPTER III

THE TRANSITION TO ACTIVE LIFE

ON leaving college the student enters the sphere of practical work. The first thing necessary is, undoubtedly, for him to gain some experience in a parish, the parish being the unit of Christian life for us in England and in the English Church. But even from the beginning students will tend to divide themselves into two classes ; one will show more practical ability, another more power of dealing with theories. The first will by preference get his material from intercourse with men and in the present ; the second will rather gather his data from history or philosophical opinion. The one will prefer direct dealing with concrete facts ; the other will find himself more able to deal with abstractions drawn from those facts. Each method has its special value, and, if our examination of the foreign and nonconforming schools of Pastoral Theology was sound, the English Church offers a special opportunity both for those who more naturally incline to historical study and to tracing out the continuous activities of spiritual life, and for those whose interest lies in direct observation and in immediate co-operation with living forces. But each study must be pursued in relation to the other; each has its peculiar value and its own difficulties.

Two classes of students.

I

The transition to active life.

Special difficulties meet the student in his passing from college to active life, some accidental, some inherent in the situation. He will be tempted to divert his attention from Pastoral Theology, because, as we saw, the way is not clear and the field is occupied by rival claimants to his interest. He must continue his theological reading, and there exist books and institutions to help him to do this which have all the prestige of a well-ordered science. Also there are activities and vigorous organizations calling for help which have all the attraction of actuality but can hardly be considered scientific. He has, therefore, a hard battle to fight if he is to be a pioneer in the new field of Pastoral Theology and an explorer in an undeveloped land. To steer his course between the two without neglecting the claims of either is a difficult task.

The change to self-direction.

This difficulty, it is to be hoped, will be lessened and removed in time, but there will always remain those which are inevitably bound up with the transition. The student who leans to the theoretical side will, after being guided by others, find the change to self-direction hard. He will not be able to avoid the natural problem of rearranging all that his mind has acquired, and of gradually building up his ideas round centres of thought that are so different from those of the mass of men around him. He has to form his habits of work, to gather together his library, to codify his notes, and to form his methods. Moreover, things always turn out different from our expectations ; the mornings when work was to be done, the rainy days when arrears were to be worked off, pass by with results quite other than those we had anticipated ; schemes of reading break down, plans fail, and results do not come out. The student slowly learns to take his own measure, to realize his limitations, to learn how long things take him to do. He has to find out at what hours he works best, what is his particular way of seeing things, what is his capacity of co-operation with others. He goes out proud, maybe, in the certainty that he has been entrusted with more than one talent to trade with, full of hope that he may have been granted five, only to find out slowly, by the hard logic of facts, that, after all, he has only been dowered with two. He has to learn to take his place as an inferior, if it must be so, without bitterness or disappointment.[1] There is, therefore, all the more necessity for him to have a foundation of habit, and of scientific habit, in his nature as opposed to custom of mere external rules. His previous life in the college is the key to the whole problem.

This natural difficulty is in present circumstances

[1] Cp. Phillips Brooks, *Twenty Sermons*. Sermon XI, ' The man with Two Talents,' p. 192 (Macmillan, 1887).

further accentuated by the demand made on his time. While it is right that he should undergo his apprenticeship in detailed work in the parish, this interferes with work on a broader scale such as this class of student is best fitted for. At present, with the exception of a few scholastic posts, there is no opening for the clergyman other than that of the ordinary curacy. There is, therefore, an imperative need for the development of different types among the clergy, and of different openings in diocesan and specialized areas to provide square holes for square pegs.

The change from theory to practice.

The other inevitable difficulty, felt perhaps more keenly by the student of the second class, is that of the transition from abstract to concrete, from books to men, from study of the history of the Prayer Book to the actual conduct of worship, from ethics to practical advice, from the theory of education to class teaching. He has to learn to be ' matter-of-fact.' Where before in summing up the results of his reading his powers of expression were only exercised in words, he has now to learn to translate conviction into action, to carry out plans when they are formed, and to say nothing till he can do something. So many people can see what should be done, but find their creative energies exhausted by verbal expression.[1] He will

[1] Cp. G. Lanson, *Histoire de la Littérature Française*, 4th ed., p. 172 : ' S'est-il (François Villon) donc corrigé ? J'avoue que je n'en crois rien : mais ce n'est pas la première fois que

find, first with surprise and then with despair, that it is one thing to get people to agree that a thing ought to be done, and quite another to get them to do it, or even to consent to its being attempted. He will discover that resolutions are passed at meetings which no one will move a step to carry out ; that when people are with difficulty convinced, the whole work has to be done over again, because they see no necessity of acting on their convictions if doing so would lead them out of their accustomed routine. He will gradually come to know what can be done and what is chimerical. He will only slowly gain confidence and

les habitudes mènent l'homme par des chemins opposés à ceux qu'indique l'aspiration momentanée de l'âme. On désire, on promet, et l'on fait le contraire. . . . Hier et tout le passé sont plus forts qu'aujourd'hui, pour donner sa forme à demain. Plus faible encore est une âme de poète que nos âmes à nous. Pour nous l'action seule réalise nos intimes pensées : le poète leur donne réalité, et mieux, éternité, par son œuvre. Quoi d'étonnant si ses plus vifs, ses plus impérieux mouvements, aussitôt exprimés, passent ? Ne doit-il pas lui sembler qu'il a agi ? ' (Did he—François Villon—reform ? I must own I do not believe it ; but this is not the first time that habit has led men by roads other than those which the soul's transient aspiration has pointed out. We desire, we promise—and we do the opposite. . . . Yesterday and the past are stronger than to-day to shape the morrow. And the poet's soul is weaker than ours. For us action alone makes real our inmost thoughts ; the poet gives them reality, nay, makes them immortal, by his work. What wonder, then, if his most vital, his most imperious inner motions pass away as soon as uttered ! Must it not seem to him that he too has done his deed ?)

acquire practical judgement. He will meet with shocks to sentiment, and experience frequent disillusionment, especially in his first two years of work. He will be tempted to despair, or take refuge in cynicism ; but he will not go under,—all this will not hurt him, will only forge his character to strength, if the scientific temper be there with the knowledge, patience, and confidence that it gives.

Need for different grades among the clergy.
This growth in ability and experience must of necessity be long and slow ; there is, therefore, all the more necessity for established grades among the clergy.[1] At present the mass are divided into vicars and curates. The former are overworked and burdened with responsibilities for which no one man can be sufficient ; the latter are denied opportunity for initiative, are all placed on a level, and get little training in management such as will fit them for independence later on. Moreover, all are not fitted by nature to rule, even were there cures enough for all. There is, therefore, an imperative need for some method of testing ability, some system of granting certificates for special study or testimonials for courses of practical training, some plan of keeping a

[1] Cp. Hooker, *Eccles. Pol.*, Book III, ch. xi. 20 : ' In performance whereof (of public religious duties) because all that are of the Church cannot jointly and equally work, the first thing in polity required is a difference of persons in the Church without which difference those functions cannot in orderly sort be executed.'

dossier of each priest which will secure a definite position to the more experienced among the unbeneficed, for some formal recognition of such qualifications so as to ensure a greater scope for their activity, and for some general policy to bring about a greater differentiation in their ranks and specialization in their work.

To whichever class the student belongs he must be ready to pay the price for efficiency. If he is of the first, he must be prepared for the isolation of mind that is the lot of all who voyage ' through strange seas of thought alone ', a solitariness that becomes harder to bear because devotion to any cause inevitably drains all the springs of a man's life to itself, makes him conscious that he is becoming warped and one-sided, absorbs interest that might have exercised itself elsewhere, and demands the renunciation of much that is innocent, desirable, and of worth, in itself. Or, if his gifts send him to direct and practical work, if he is to keep the power of perceiving what men think and feel, if he is to train the instinct by which he may judge the finer things of their lives, he must count the cost to be paid in the sensitiveness that is its inevitable accompaniment; [1] he must be prepared to come into close contact with vulgarity and

Paying the price.

---

[1] Cp. *The Life of Charlotte Yonge*, by C. Coleridge, p. 129. ' She told me once that Mr. Keble had told her that forecasting and terrors for those we loved was the price paid for having an imagination.'

coarseness without learning to mind it one whit the less, to be encountered by acrid opposition or stolid indifference without becoming unsympathetic, to see vice familiarly at close quarters under the show of respectability without losing his horror of it, to see the inevitable future without becoming unbalanced in mind, to move in an atmosphere of mean and sordid aims without losing faith in those who are so often actuated by them, to know man as he is but always to see him as he may be. He will have to mind what people think and feel about him, and at the same time, when necessary, absolutely to disregard it, not even let them realize that he knows and sees it all.

II

The student ideal. The interests of the student of Pastoral Theology may lead him to the theoretical or to the practical side of the science, but in any case the work of one kind must be in touch with that of the other, and he must remain a student through life. The aim of his training in the Theological College, and in his apprenticeship in the parish, is to create an ideal which in its qualities is the same for both types, though it differs in the matter with which they have to do.

Continuity of thought. Scientific training of the student will ensure a continuity of thought which will gradually transform the nature of parish work. He will begin to arrange his work on a more continuous plan. He will have learned to see things steadily. He will not be content with sermons arranged for during the week before they are preached, but will, in his own mind at least, thread them together to form a continuous scheme of teaching. He will form plans of study or of practical under-takings, instead of doing things as they arise. By this means he will be able to test them by continuous observation, and to introduce a purpose into all his work. He will always ask himself what he is aiming at, and will be able to tell after a fair trial whether an undertaking is worth going on with or whether it may as well be dropped. This will produce in him a new attitude towards tradition, on which so much of our present work is based ; he will learn to value it more because it witnesses to a continuous life, but at the same time he will be more ready to depart from it as soon as he has built up something new to substitute for its old-fashioned methods. He will criticize by construction and build up before destroying. By the habit of continuous thought he will turn his experiences into experience. He will gain the power to specialize by sustained attention, and will be continually increasing his qualifications in his science.

Scientific training will also give him a wider view. He will learn to correlate the various activities in his parish, first in his own mind, and

Width of view.

then by actual co-ordination. Instead of letting each go its own way without regard to the others, he will watch for their interaction on one another. His sermons will no longer be isolated discourses, but will take their place in the scheme of things, supporting and enforcing a policy. He will see the life of the local church as a unity, and will set himself to make its elements combine. He will believe in organization, understanding that only organic things have life.[1] He will not only see things steadily, but will see them whole. He will also see the parish in relation to the Church of which it is a part. He will be prepared for inter-parochial action and study. He will be ready to apply scientific methods tested in the parish to the larger area of the diocese. He will be able, and anxious, to work with other students, a thing necessary for all effective or sound work, and will be prepared, if necessary, to do the preliminary research on which others may build the final result.

He will be no less ready to note the relation of the Church to the world. He will have eyes to see just where men need the help of Christianity, just where they want the Christian inter-

---

[1] There is widespread prejudice against the word ' organization ' due to a general misunderstanding of its meaning. A ' well-organized parish ' only too often means one in which there exists a mass of uncorrelated activities overlapping one another, each with its own machinery, and exhausting the energies of the workers by its lack of organic unity.

pretation of their lives. He will acquire the
faculty of distinguishing types of men, of knowing
instinctively what special element they lack which
the Gospel can supply. He will learn to penetrate
with a specialist's accuracy to the moral issues
involved in questions arising on the stage, in
books, round politics, or from society. He will
come more and more to understand men in their
complicated lives, and find points of contact
which a weak emotional ' sympathy ' cannot
supply. He will be able, that is, to correlate
Pastoral Theology with other inferior, though
better worked out, sciences.

He will have the same unity in himself. The
ideal student will be the ' foursquare man ' who
will ' bear the chances of life nobly with perfect
and complete harmony '.[1] He will be consistent
rather than versatile, able to work in any direction
because he has correlated all his own faculties and
has a base from which to start this way or that.
He will become the efficient man, the man people
trust and consult. A more thorough training will
result in an increased variety among the clergy,
with a consequent increased power of acting on
different lines and in different areas, but with a
common basis of scientific method that will enable

The four-square man.

[1] Cp. Aristotle, *Eth. Nic.* i. 10 : καὶ τὰς τύχας οἴσει κάλλιστα
καὶ πάντῃ πάντως ἐμμελῶς ὅ γ᾽ ὡς ἀληθῶς ἀγαθὸς καὶ τετράγωνος ἄνευ
ψόγου. Dante, *Par.* xvii. 24 : ' Ben tetragono ai colpi di
ventura.' (Well squared to fortune's blows.)

them to co-operate. It will make available an enlarged area of observation of the facts of spiritual life, and give an increased value to conference. It will extend the influence of the clergy in a way legitimate and welcome, but all this depends on their being scientific students of Pastoral Theology on their realizing the need of theory and its connexion with practice.

BOOK III

THE SCOPE OF PASTORAL THEOLOGY

' I look upon all the world as my parish.'—*On the Monument to the Wesleys in Westminster Abbey.*

CHAPTER I

PASTORAL THEOLOGY AND PSYCHOLOGY

WE are now in a position to go on to consider the task of the actual construction of a School of Pastoral Theology, to examine what is included in the whole area of investigation, how the different parts may be unified and their connexion with one another shown, and how the general laws which work in the whole field may be discovered.

In considering the subject-matter of a science the first step is to examine its relation to other sciences. This involves more than mere definition ; we have to note where they overlap and what is their common ground. We have already done this in the case of Theology of which Pastoral Theology is a department, but there remain three which are closely allied to it, namely, Psychology, Education, and Sociology. With these it has large areas in common, and we need to study them so that, in isolating our special subject, we may know that we are isolating it, that we may avoid devoting

Relation to other sciences.

K 2

our attention to any of them under the impression that they are parts of Pastoral Theology, that we may see how one science helps any one of the others and is in turn helped by it.

Impor-
tance of
Psycho-
logy.

The importance of the study of Psychology has long been recognized in matters of Education ; its special features when dealing with the child have been detailed in many excellent books and the results used in their work by the great body of teachers.   Lately, too, much interest has been taken in its theological aspect, and the psychology of religious experience has attracted considerable attention.   But there has not been the same use made of its conclusions for practical purposes in the parish, though obviously its laws must concern our action there.   Moreover, there is a large field for the study of religion in its normal existence, while hitherto attention has chiefly been directed to the abnormal manifestations which force themselves on public notice.   The relation of Psychology and Pastoral Theology, therefore, needs to be more closely examined.

What
may be
omitted.

It is not, perhaps, necessary for the student of the latter to study minutely the physical basis of the former science, but he must recognize its existence as it affects many things with which he deals.   Physical changes modify spiritual developments.   The change to manhood obviously influences religious life, whether it produces the phenomena of conversion, or is accompanied by an

orderly resettlement of belief and practice. The
life of the soul has to go on through times of ill
health, and this presents a practical problem
related to, but different from, that of explaining
how sickness influences the inner man. To
realize the natural laws governing the recurrent
periods of spiritual dryness, so often alluded to
in the *Imitatio Christi* and by all masters of
Ascetic Theology, will comfort the person who
experiences them. A clear knowledge of the
temporary exhaustion of will power that follows
the stimulus of public speaking will help us to
understand the strange moral collapse of some
of those who have preached to others, and will
make the preacher himself forewarned and fore-
armed against the danger. With a slight knowledge of physical processes it becomes much easier
in hours of gloom to fulfil ' tasks in hours of
insight willed '.[1]

Again, a detailed study of the psychology of
sensation is not necessary for the student of
Pastoral Theology, though it may prove a valuable
training to him in the idea of law ; and, since
the senses are the avenues of temptation, such
a study may be useful in casuistry and for the purposes of guiding men.[2] It is rather in the ordinary

[1] Matthew Arnold, *Morality*.

[2] It was in this way that St. Augustine, in writing his Confessions, analysed in the tenth book the temptations of touch,
taste, smell, hearing, and sight, with a deliberate intention of
helping others.

sphere of pastoral work that the value of a study of Psychology will appear. There are a number of familiar facts that can be easily referred to certain well-known laws, and will become much more intelligible by being so referred ; there are many laws established on other grounds which may, when realized, greatly modify our accepted methods ; and there are many widespread features of religious life which are not fully understood, since the laws which govern them have still to be sought.

I

Familiar facts referred to simple laws— attention.

To take first familiar facts which can be referred to simple laws, such as those of attention and fatigue. It is a noteworthy fact that public services always tend to last about an hour and a quarter. If they are longer people are inclined to come late ; if they are shorter, as in the case of plain celebrations of the Eucharist, an instinct makes it natural to come to church from five minutes to a quarter of an hour before, and to stay the same time after the service.[1] So on a week-day evening more people come when Evensong is followed by a sermon or a Guild Office. It does not seem worth while to come for the Office

---

[1] This instinct has been generally thwarted in England by locked doors, but its influence can be clearly observed in Roman Catholic countries.

by itself.   This probably is not consciously thought out, but the half-hour service leaves a feeling of incompleteness which is acted upon instinctively. Similarly, the less varied interest of a well-delivered sermon preached by itself gets exhausted in about fifty minutes, the normal length of a college lecture or of an act in a three-act play.   If, however, the sermon is merely a single element in public worship, attention begins to relax after about twenty minutes, just as a speaker at a public dinner where there is also music and conversation begins to bore his hearers if he exceeds that limit.

Attention, it is well known, can be stimulated by expectation.   In the case of an irregularly recurring noise, such as that caused by the explosions of a gas engine, or by a boy crying papers, this can become so powerful as to prevent any fixing of the mind on other subjects.   So the waiting for the sound of the sacring bell in the Roman Mass has a powerful effect in welding a heterogeneous crowd of men into a unity in worship when they are

> All famishing in expectation
> Of the main altar's consummation.[1]

The effect is no doubt incidental, not deliberate ; the kind of attention may, or may not, be the right one ; the means of securing it can be deprecated or justified ; but the fact is one of experience.   Similar working of the same law may

---

[1] Browning, *Christmas Eve*, x.

be found in revival meetings, where intense interest
is excited by watching to see who will go up next
to the ' penitent form ', or how many will stand up
to testify to their conversion.

Attention can also be fixed by other means.
The effect of lights, or of repetition of single
phrases or actions, is well known to all who have
studied the phenomena of hypnotism. The use
of altar lights, though perhaps historically due to
tradition, has, it may be argued, a definite sym-
bolical value ; but it also most probably has a
considerable influence in aiding the worshipper to
concentrate his attention on the service. The
repetition of words and actions in the use of the
Rosary helps to make the mind of the user oblivious
to distracting sensations, so that his thoughts are
more easily fixed on the mystery contemplated.
Again, it is difficult to decide how far these customs
are, or are not, justifiable, though the parallel use
of rhythmical sounds in hymn-singing and other
forms of music is accepted without question, and
litanies based on the recurrence of refrains constitute a recognized classic form of devotion.
The use made in certain forms of evangelical effort
of the repetition of texts,[1] of invitations to come
forward, or of a sung refrain, often accompanied
by gestures and motions of the arms similar to
those employed in hypnotism, would appear to

[1] For a classic example of the obsession due to the continual repetition of texts see Bunyan's *Grace Abounding*.

be less capable of justification, but none of these questions can be fairly discussed or decided without realizing the existence of the laws on which the phenomena are based.

The laws of fatigue form part of the study of attention. Variation and contrast in the objects presented to the mind enable us to maintain our interest in them. The intensity of this interest regularly affects our power of sustaining it. Continuous illustration of this principle may be found in public worship. 'Forasmuch as effectual prayer is joined with a vehement intention of the inferior powers of the soul, which cannot therein long continue without pain, it hath been therefore thought good so by turns to interpose still somewhat for the higher part of the mind, the understanding, to work upon, that both being kept in continual exercise with variety, neither might feel any great weariness, and yet each be a spur to the other.'[1] The alternation of prayers and lessons, whether reasoned or growing up instinctively, is based upon this law of fatigue, and is but one illustration of a principle that underlies the whole art and science of Liturgiology, that guides all instincts as to the amount of variation needed, that decides the relative fitness of ' free prayer ' or fixed forms, that demands a simple structure of worship to balance the variety of the one, and increases the unvarying and familiar

Fatigue.

[1] Hooker, *Eccles. Pol.*, Book V, ch. xxxiv, § 1.

elements of a liturgical service in proportion to
its elaboration.[1]

Habit.   The psychology of habit finds obvious illustrations in normal religious life.   Long ago Bishop
Butler [2] pointed out that 'practical habits are
formed and strengthened by repeated acts, and
that passive impressions grow weaker by being
repeated on us', and used the facts for apologetic
purposes to support the belief that in this world
we are in a state of probation.   But its laws are
illustrated even more clearly in pastoral work.
They illuminate many features in the whole wide
question of the balance of the evangelical and
ritual elements in religion, by showing them to be
not arbitrary but based on the nature of man.
The length of time it takes for habits to grow
decides the period required for new customs to
be accepted, for a congregation to be built up,
for influence to tell, for an established organization, such as a boys' class, to become permanent.
The variations in town and country in the rate
of change of habits, and consequently of their
permanence or growth, must be reckoned with.
The possibility of their being continued under
changed conditions must be considered, especially

[1] Readers of Harold Frederic's unpleasing story *Illumination* will remember how Sister Soulsby, the 'debt raiser',
riveted the attention of her congregation by singing the
familiar words of the hymn 'Rock of Ages' to the unfamiliar
tune of one of Chopin's mazurkas.

[2] *Analogy*, ch. v.

when we are dealing with children, or others, who are being trained in institutions or under special circumstances.[1]

The laws of association are more complicated, and therefore find more frequent illustration in Pastoral Theology. For instance, the rapidity with which we can reproduce the connexion of a word and idea varies with its familiarity. A speaker in a foreign language always seems to speak more rapidly ; to make himself understood to us he must talk slowly. In public worship this law must govern the pace at which the various parts of the service may be read. Complaints of indistinctness and rapidity will always come from those to whom the whole is strange. The familiar, unchanging prayers can be said quite rapidly in a low voice without becoming inaudible or seeming to be gabbled, especially on a week-day when none are present but frequent church-goers ; changing parts, such as the Epistle and Gospel, must be read with more distinctness and more slowly. In sermons difficult or unfamiliar thoughts demand a slower delivery. In the same way the laws of association of ideas with acts form the basis on which ceremonial is built up as wordless language ; they provide principles by which the

Associa-
tion.

---

[1] At present we are taking great pains to train girls of the working classes in habits of worship at 11 a.m. on Sunday morning, which in the circumstances of their adult life the great majority will never be able to practise.

value or danger of external religion may be judged ;
they underlie all questions of symbol and sacrament.   Many customs of Lent and of fast days,
often trivial in themselves, can be justified on the
ground that they create artificial and deliberate
associations of things of everyday life, even such
as smoking or taking sugar in tea, with great
religious ideas.   The conception of consecration of
times and places can be explained by scientific
psychological laws ;   guided by them we see a
reason why the ' cella continuata dulcescit ',[1] and
why choirs should not be allowed to practise in
the   chancel ;   the   question   whether   reverence
should, or should not, be paid to material objects
can   be   argued   on   reasonable   grounds ;   and
explanation can be found for the feeling that in
certain churches it is natural to pray.

II

Estab-
lished
laws in-
fluenc-
ing
methods.

The above illustrations, which might easily be
multiplied, are comparatively simple.   They deal
with familiar facts, which can with little difficulty
be referred to elementary laws of sensation and
perception.   When we pass on to the more complex problems of man's whole nature, of the rela-

----

[1] Cp. À Kempis, *De Imitatione Christi*, Lib. I, cap. xx :
' In cella invenies, quod deforis saepius amittes.   Cella
continuata dulcescit, et male custodita taedium generat.
Si in principio conversionis tuae bene illam incolueris et
custodieris, erit tibi postea dilecta amica et gratissimum

tions of feeling, understanding, and will, to one another, the corresponding laws of Pastoral Theology are less easily noted, but just because we are in danger of overlooking them, to search for signs of their working will make us more cautious in forming conclusions, and when they are discovered they will often compel us greatly to modify our action.

In studying the physical basis of Psychology the chief interest lies in the fact that sensations are connected with motions in certain nerve centres, and (in the area common to it and Pastoral Theology) in the realization that the vigour of spiritual life is regularly influenced by bodily conditions. But the question of the reactions of mind and matter on one another presents a whole series of far more difficult problems which need to be carefully studied. In the medical world the value of suggestion, especially in the cure of nervous disorders, is being given due consideration, and we are witnessing a great extension of interest in faith-healing in various forms among religious people ; but in both these cases men are dealing with persons already ill from other causes. *Body and spirit.*

solacium.' (In thy chamber thou shalt find what abroad thou shalt too often lose. The more thou visitest thy chamber the more thou wilt enjoy it ; the less thou comest thereto, the more will it weary thee. If in the beginning of thy conversion thou art content to remain in it, and keep to it well, it will afterwards be to thee a dear friend and a most pleasant comfort.)

The question of how bodily evil is caused by the action of the mind before the person in question is recognized as disordered, the relation of the oncoming of insanity to sin, the stereotyping of bodily changes by acts of drunkenness or sexual vice which gradually enslave the will, and morbid conditions brought about by indulged anger, laziness, jealousy, or religious bigotry, all need to be scientifically examined in the area of normal religious life if penitents are to be saved from turning into patients.

Emotion, intellect, and will.   The order of development of the different elements of religious life as conditioned by the natural growth of the body, as well as the influence of a Christian life on physical development, is a matter which belongs rather to the science of education.   But the psychology of the emotions, the intellect and the will (to use the ordinary terms of everyday speech) present to us many laws both of their distinct features and of their interaction on one another, which will, if realized, prove invaluable in practical pastoral work.   The relatively strong impulse of certain sensations, and their short duration, should obviously be borne in mind when, for instance, music plays such a large part in public worship, and will explain why continually, from the time of Plato to the present day, ' the introduction of a new kind of music will be shunned as imperilling the whole state, since styles of music are never disturbed without affecting the most important political institutions.' [1] In matters of intellect, to take one example, the psychology of doubt has a patent bearing on Pastoral Theology, for it must be understood if we are to ' argue ' properly with people. In the sphere of the will the value and nature of individual influence presents a puzzle only partially worked out in Psychology, yet whole areas of practical undertakings—for example visiting 'to break down prejudice', clubs 'to get hold of the men ', direction of penitents, and all that is vaguely called ' personal work '—are covered with institutions that are based on laws very imperfectly understood.

In the interaction of these faculties similar problems present themselves. The balance of the emotions and understanding in song is a delicate matter, yet its laws govern the whole question of the rival claims of music and words in worship, and present immediate difficulties in such matters as customs of chanting or habits of organists. The power of the intellect over the feelings and will must be rightly estimated before we can judge how far, and how soon, people are influenced by ideas, a question on which our whole conception of apologetic and policy of evangelization must be based. A reconsideration of the subject is going on in the worlds of business and politics, with wide-reaching results in methods of advertise-

[1] *Republic,* Book IV. 424 c.

ment and electioneering ;[1] for the Church the natural difficulty of such reconstruction is increased by her moral responsibility, since she has to consider how far various methods are justified as well as whether they are successful. The mutual relation of word and idea varies in different people, classes, and nations, in a way hardly suspected by any but the trained observer, yet it must certainly be known if we are rightly to value professions of faith (which may strengthen the will of some, and encourage hypocrisy in others), or if missionaries are to build up their work on sure ground. The dissolution of the normal connexion of thought, impulse, and will, in dreams, often causes real anxiety of conscience, and entails serious trouble to right-minded men, to meet which with wisdom it is clearly necessary to understand the psychological conditions of sleeping states.

Universal laws. There are certain laws of human nature which are universal. These are often rather assumed and gauged instinctively than reasoned out. The whole fabrics of society, of commerce, and of politics, are based on the assumption that within certain limits men are the same everywhere. The study of Psychology detects signs of similar laws in the spiritual sphere and in the fabric of pastoral work. Such, for instance, seem to underlie the

[1] Cp. Graham Wallas, *Human Nature in Politics* (Constable & Co., 1908), especially p. 196.

conception of worship. They can be traced as natural human instincts among savage races in the past. They find expression in varied forms of religion. The early Christians could only explain the similarity of their rites, independently evolved, to those of the traditions of the heathen by attributing the latter to the malignant imitation of demons. Many features of Buddhist worship are identical with those of Western Christendom. The Roman Catholic Mass is found practically the same in all parts of the world, and responds to the religious needs of people as different as are the Irish and the Swiss, the Italians and the Dutch, the Germans and the men of Peru, the Indians and the Chinese; it unites all classes and both sexes in a great democracy of common feeling, thought, and action. Moreover, rightly or wrongly, a form of worship in all essentials precisely similar has revived in the English Church among people the vast majority of whom have never witnessed the Roman rite, and have even been trained by tradition and precept to regard it as superstitious; while among the masses of our countrymen who have witnessed neither, certain cadences, tones of chanting, scents of burning gums, shapes of vestments, motions of worshippers, lines of architecture, appeal at once, on their first presentation, to their religious sense, when put before them in show on the boards of the stage. Clearly here we have some great human instinct which, whether it should be satisfied or repressed, trained or rooted up, we ignore at our peril.

A similar law can be traced in the hardly less popular form of churchgoing that centres round preaching, which appears among the Germans, the Dutch, the Scotch, English Nonconformists, in University sermons, and Roman Catholic and other missions, and presents a type to which 'special services' in the English Church perpetually tend to recur. Another example of an almost universal religious instinct can be found in the custom of pilgrimages, which can be traced from the times of Abercius and Hegesippus[1] through the Middle Ages down to its curious transformation in the shape of the modern Sunday school treat and parish outing.

Just as, on the one side, we can rely on certain instincts which seem to be common to all men, we often err on the other by ignoring differences in individuals and races. If some practices may claim to be catholic because based on the common element in human nature, certain devotions are not natural or good for all men. The problem of distinguishing between the two classes is one of delicate observation and religious sensibility, and is quite ignored by our rough and ready criteria in the present day ; yet on it depends the whole question of publication, diffusion, and use, of devotional literature.

[1] Eus., *Hist. Eccles.*, Book. IV, ch. xxii.

The pathological side of the study of the psycho- *Patho-* logy of religion plays an important part in *logy.* Pastoral Theology. Though this is the aspect of the subject that has received most attention of recent years, there is still much to do. Obscure laws of morbid conditions seem to exist, such, for example, as that which sometimes reveals itself in a curious combination of an obsessing interest in ritual, or of an eager desire to preach in public, with perverted instincts. These laws ought to be realized so that sympathetic and firm treatment may be at once adopted for those who suffer under them. As a part of casuistry knowledge of such laws is needed for dealing with individuals, but in organized ministerial work also the problems raised by the existence of such persons have to be faced.

III

There are also features of religious life which *Features* are familiar but are not fully understood or noted, *and* and are difficult to examine because the psycho- *laws im-* logical laws to which they may be referred still *ly under-* require much study and elaboration. Here *stood.* Pastoral Theology will often be able to contribute useful material as well as to reap profit for its own undertakings.

From the fact that it deals with one of the most *The* widespread and vigorous expressions of corporate *logy* life, it has exceptional opportunities for studying the *of the crowd;*

' psychology of the crowd ', in other words the way in which the impressions and acts of individuals are modified by the presence of a mass of their fellow men when they are all being worked on by the same influence and are acting in a similar way. This is in accordance with certain definite principles by which peculiarities are inhibited and common impulses stimulated. On these laws much of the art of rhetoric has been built up both empirically and scientifically, and preaching is, if not the most popular, at least the most widespread form of the art. Its limitations are perhaps more clearly realized after a study of the psychological aspect of the question, and this may prove of value in correcting an exaggerated estimate of its effectiveness, both on the part of the preacher, who is liable to overvalue it because he is misled by his natural feeling of excitement in moving a mass of people, and on the part of those who view it from outside, see the immediate effects, and build up a whole theory of pastoral method which they would revise if they had opportunities of testing its value. Similarly the laws of common action provide some of the fundamental principles of common worship ; the difference of private and public prayer, the need of greater simplicity in language in which all men join, the greater elaboration of ceremonial possible when men act socially, the power of common thought to dignify plain, sometimes even weak, expressions which would be bald and inadequate in private use, the justification of antiphonal chanting, part-singing, and orchestration, are all matters of the science of Liturgiology, but must be studied on a basis of psychological laws. No less important is it to study the abnormal forms of the action of the crowd as exhibited in re-vivalism. About these there is a large amount of empirical knowledge, much of which has been published in handbooks, but the danger, both mental and moral, of the experiments suggested, often, it would seem, with little understanding of the great forces being set in motion, seems hardly to be realized.

The psychology of sex has also an intimate of sex. connexion with pastoral work. Perhaps here attention has been too exclusively directed to the question of sex attraction. This is important, no doubt, and should be borne in mind. It should not be assumed, for instance, that ' women teachers are much the best for young lads' classes ', without careful consideration of all that is involved. Again, the existence of perverted instincts should be recognized and guarded against, even if it need not be discussed. But more important, if only because of the extent of their influence, are the ordinary laws according to which men and women differ. The relative part which emotion plays in the one and the other and the relative force which it exerts, the peculiar preferences of

either sex,[1] the difference in the development of
boys and girls, the greater interest in, and capacity
for, detail shown by women, and for policy and
administration by men, should be reckoned with,
since on them depend whole questions of special
services and methods for each sex (whether
advisable, or tending to emphasize one-sided conceptions), of preparation for confirmation and
dealing with the recasting of religious belief and
practice, of church government and of the whole
conception of ' church work '.

To take a single example. It will be noticed
that where left to themselves men, if they wish
to be undistracted, invariably get together. Even
though non-smokers, they often prefer to travel
in smoking-carriages. At parties a good hostess
has to prevent their converging. At public
meetings or lectures they congregate at the back
of the room and, by preference, stand or sit
with their backs to the wall. So in all churches,
where they are not artificially forced by pews and
pew rents to ' sit with their families ', or by
officious vergers to occupy seats in front, they
prefer to remain at the bottom of the church and
to stand. The instinct seems to be universal
at any rate all over Europe. Obviously where it

[1] These are quite different questions, though it is generally
assumed that because women are normally guided more by
their emotions, which may, or may not, be the case, that they
therefore have them less under control and that those of men
are less violent and irregular.

is ignored, as in most English churches, the price has to be paid.

The whole question of the development of the different faculties, and of the order in which they mature, is equally important. The larger matters of human life and civilization raise many questions of even greater interest, but these belong rather to the sciences of education and of sociology, and must be considered separately from the study of the relation of Psychology to Pastoral Theology.

CHAPTER II

PASTORAL THEOLOGY AND EDUCATION

Teaching part of pastoral work.

TEACHING has always been recognized as an integral part of pastoral work. The Early Church took her share in the education of the people of the ancient world,[1] and the Catechetical School at Alexandria upheld an ideal which has perhaps never been surpassed in modern times.[2] The Emperor Julian saw that, for the extermination of Christianity which he desired, his strongest weapon was what would nowadays be called the ' laicization of the schools '. Augustine wrote one of his most-read works on Christian teaching. In the Dark Ages the *schola cantorum* of Gregory and the monasteries of the Benedictines maintained the tradition of the old civilization in the West. The schools of Theodore and Hadrian at Canterbury, of Benedict Biscop at Wearmouth and Jarrow, of Alcuin and Karl the Great, prepared the way for the rise of the mediaeval universities,[3] and the

[1] Cp. G. Hodgson, *Primitive Christian Education* (T. & T. Clark, 1906).

[2] Cp. Greg. Thaum. *Oratio Panegyrica*, quoted in B. F. Westcott, *Religious Thought in the West*, p. 214, ' Origen and the Beginnings of Christian Philosophy ' (Macmillan, 1891).

[3] Cp. Bede, *Hist. Eccles.*, Lib. IV, cap. ii, and Introd., p. xvii, of C. Plummer's Oxford edition. J. Bass Mullinger, Art. ' Schools ' in *Dict. Christ. Ant.*

enthusiasm of the Friars christianized scholastic philosophy. The Jesuits and the men of Port Royal in the seventeenth century were the pioneers of many of our modern educational ideals, and, while Fénelon and Mme. de Maintenon made their schemes for the education of women in the upper classes, La Salle and the Christian Brothers initiated the elementary education now compulsory in most civilized countries. In our own land the public and grammar schools were founded in intimate association with the Church; the experiment of Wesley at Kingswood, though not immediately successful, represented a new and bold attempt to face the problem afresh; the great movement for the education of the masses, associated with the names of the National Society and with the British Schools, was primarily a religious one, and the Oxford Movement owed no small share of its power to the fact that it was largely an educational reform, bringing in a new and more human conception of the duties of tutors to their pupils and of the mutual relations of teacher and taught. To this day successful schoolmasters are often made bishops.

But, throughout the past, religion has been regarded mainly as a factor in education. Important and necessary as is this aspect, it is only one way of considering its energy. Education has been treated as a separate science since Locke and Rousseau wrote, and as one that included religious

Mutual relationships to be studied.

teaching ; but there has been no corresponding consideration of the Pastoral Science which includes education as one element in its whole field. The common ground of the two sciences has not been marked off and investigated in relation to the two larger wholes. Pastoral Theology has lagged behind in the scientific advance of recent years, to the great injury of religious teaching and to the one-sided development of pedagogy. There is immediate need, therefore, for a scientific treatment of both, independently and in their relationships to one another.

I

Secular and religious lessons.

The first thing to do is to define the areas of pastoral work and education, or at least to see in what sense they can be divided. It is often said that ' there is no such thing as denominational arithmetic ', and of arithmetic viewed purely in the abstract the statement is true. Twice two is four to the Christian and to the atheist. But, as a practical matter, in the teaching of arithmetic the spirit in which it is taught is of great consequence. The personality of the teacher counts, and the lesson cannot be dissociated from the whole course or from the school in which it is given. It is bad pedagogy to ignore the fact. The definition which declares arithmetic and drawing to be secular, and history and Scripture to be religious, is based on abstractions which, though they may be valid mentally and logically, have no counterpart in real life. Every lesson in a Christian school is a religious lesson. The same qualities of sincerity and care are needed for every subject ; that is, no part of the area of education is untouched by religion, and none can be withdrawn from Pastoral Theology.

It follows from this that the same methods that are insisted on in other subjects must be applied in practice to the lessons which are essentially and logically religious. At present, as a result of the isolation of pastoral work, obsolete and amateur methods obtain in the teaching it undertakes. We teach catechisms by heart ; we reward by marks, often unsystematically and irregularly given ; we rely for interest on treats and prizes, our fundamental assumption being that learning is something wearisome and disagreeable that must be compensated for ; there is an almost entire absence of paper-work and systematic questioning, little or no use of pictures or objects round which lessons are given. We make children shout answers in unison, and accustom them to do this in church. We allow them to sing doggerel hymns to vulgar tunes which would never be tolerated for one instant by His Majesty's inspectors of schools, and we justify our practice by saying that ' the children like something bright'. We ask 'elliptical' and ' Yes and No ' questions ; we make abstract

Loss to religious teaching by separation,

statements which are unintelligible to the child
mind, and explain by illustrations which do not
illustrate—all common and obvious faults which
a trained teacher would detect at once, and could
put right in a week. It is hardly too much to say
that in the ordinary Sunday school, to take the
most characteristic example of our undertakings,
the method and conception of education involved
is that of the dame's school of a hundred years
ago, the disappearance of which Wordsworth
regretted.

The unfortunate thing is that this is regarded
as natural and inevitable. There seems to be but
little consciousness that any other kind of teaching
exists. There are, it is true, signs of dissatisfaction
with the present state of affairs, and earnest
measures for improvement are in hand. Courses for
Sunday school teachers are being arranged ; im-
proved methods based on foreign models are being
introduced ; but, as a rule, even these ignore the
fact that for years in our public elementary schools
a body of devoted and trained men and women
have, day by day, been giving religious instruction
and have been carrying out the schemes that are
tentatively proposed as new ideas, and have even
come to regard them as old-fashioned and out of
date. The separation of Pastoral Theology and
professional education can perhaps hardly be better
illustrated than in this matter of Sunday schools
and public catechizing.

In many schools where teaching is given by experts the case is still far from satisfactory. In public and secondary schools the religious teaching is often reduced to a minimum in quantity, and has to be so adapted as not to offend anybody and to risk no chance of doing so. Even in elementary schools where it is given every day, and in Church schools where the teacher is free from undenominational restrictions and has a freer hand, the obsolete methods still linger. There is still far too much learning by rote, too much 'illustration by Scripture proofs'. There is a certain timidity which prevents a bold facing of such questions as, for instance, the right method of teaching the Old Testament. And this is often reinforced by the authorities, not so much of the diocese as of the county, who forbid the taking of children to church, and do nothing to encourage the giving of religious object-lessons, the employment of sacred pictures or symbols, the acquisition of theological books for the teachers' library, the holding of conferences on Christian teaching, and all the methods which a trained teacher would be only too ready to adopt. In most books on religious teaching we are conscious of a marked amateurishness. In general works on education, when we come to the chapter which deals with it, we feel that we pass into a different atmosphere, one, at best, of formal deference to the seriousness of the subject, or, more often, one of tentative

even when given by trained teachers.

suggestion or mere individual experience ; or where such books are written by experts [1] they have to be written down to the standard of the amateurs in whose hands religious teaching as a part of pastoral work mainly lies.

II

The loss to Pastoral Theology. But if the isolation of the ordinary religious teaching given in parishes and schools from the great body of educational science has unfortunate results, the loss to education as a whole through its separation from Pastoral Theology is far more serious. The great mass of books on teaching do not refer to religion at all, even in a perfunctory and tentative manner. The majority of modern French works, it is true, are permeated by a spirit actively hostile to Christianity, and deliberately propose substitutes for it, but the greater number of those written at home do not attack religion— they simply ignore it. No one can study the excellent literature that is being produced all round us—as, for instance, the Board of Education's *Suggestions for the consideration of Teachers* [2] —without becoming increasingly conscious of this defect. The symmetry of the whole is destroyed ;

[1] e.g. Miss Hetty Lee's *New Methods in the Junior Sunday School* (National Society). Prof. J. Adams' little *Primer on Teaching, with Special Reference to Sunday School Work* (T. & T. Clark), is an admirable example of first-class work adapted to popular use.

[2] Wyman & Sons, 1905.

the conception of education becomes lopsided. The gap in the scheme must entail, we feel, a corresponding deformity in the growth of the child's mind. Moreover, as religion is the one really co-ordinating element among the various subjects, the whole structure seems uncorrelated, isolated in its various elements, and ready to fall to pieces. Religion is an essential element in education ; quite apart from the truth of any particular creed, or from its necessity as a sanction of morals, simply as an instrument of culture it is more powerful than any other. The loss to those who have from motives of conscience to omit it, as well as to that large number who, from having no faith that leads to any religious practice, are out of touch with its forces, is incalculable.

Not only is it the best instrument of culture for the masses of men ; it is practically the only one available at once, of immediate interest, and able to carry on the work begun at school through their whole lives. In the teaching of language and literature children may be trained to appreciate the poetry of Shakespeare, but the words of the Bible, the prayers of public worship, the hymns they sing, the oratory of the pulpit will furnish for them their permanent standard of noble verse and prose. The political history of their country is faint in outline and difficult to grasp, while a vivid knowledge of the past will come from the story of the Chosen People, a lively sense

Religion as an instrument of education.

of far-off ages from their comparison of present
things with those done and said in ancient Pales-
tine ; the village church will be the concrete
embodiment of antiquity in their midst ; their
sense of oneness with days of long ago will spring
from their membership in an historic body whose
weekly and daily activity will always come nearer
to them than the doings of Parliament. Geography
first reaches out beyond home surroundings in the
knowledge (often undesirable knowledge) gained
by their parochial excursion, or, in a better way,
by their visit to their cathedral ; the diocese
governed by the bishop is understood as an
area more easily than the county represented by the
inspector ; while pride in the colonies of England,
coloured red on the map, is at least no surer
instrument to make them realize the peoples and
lands of the world than the inculcation of their
responsibility to the heathen by the missionary-
box, or the habit of remembering them in their
prayers. With infinite labour people are endeavouring to instil into children a love of good music,
to train taste in pictorial art, and to induce grace of
bearing by drill, country dances, and games ; but
for the masses the only music not utterly vulgar
that they will hear later on will be in church ; the
only architecture worthy of the name that they
will be familiar with will be that which sets their
feet in a large room Sunday by Sunday ; the only
pictures with a content more than merely trivial

will be the religious ones on the walls of their homes, the sculptures and frescoes, the embroideries and banners which might, at any rate, be familiar to all at their times of worship ; the only place where dignity of bearing is demanded will be the sanctuary where the roughest choir-boy is made to speak and walk with restraint. So, too, the creeds—religious or materialist—that men hold will always furnish, for good or ill, the only possible forms of popular philosophy ; their sense of solidarity, for calling out of which the constant use of the big hall in schools is recommended, will for most find no other means of being kept alive in later life than by the regularly recurring assembling of themselves together, high and low, rich and poor, one with another. When we contrast the constant opportunities for education in all these directions afforded ready to hand by the Church with the extraordinary difficulty of attaining the same results by secular means, we feel how amazing it is that any one who cares for children should even suggest the banishment of religion from the school or the relegation of its teaching to amateur effort.

Moreover, it is one subject which does all this. *Co-ordinating other subjects.* It is sometimes declared that the co-ordination of different studies is overdone, and possibly the ways in which one subject is made to back up another are often artificial and strained. But here the unification of education is natural and automatic ;

each element acts and reacts on the others ; each reinforces and gives a meaning to the rest ; and this is in itself an education, one gained in religious teaching, when not isolated from secular, with the least possible difficulty.

Educating from within.
But the matter does not end there. The religious lesson has the greatest interest, and therefore the greatest effect, because of the direct personal participation of the children in it. It is ' *our* Church, *our* Prayer Book, *our* cathedral, *our* missionary society, *our* choir, *our* services, *our* pictures, *our* creed, *our* congregation ', that they are learning about. Moreover, the ordinary lessons always remain something outside the child, something instilled *de haut en bas*. He may learn to take on his lips the words of Shakespeare and act them, to think about countries far away, to sing good songs because he is taught ; but in his religion the language of prayer comes from within, his intercession for others brings the thought of them to his heart, the music of his hymns springs from the very fount of his being, and all this, educating life at its core, works from within outward, and refines and sanctifies the whole man.

The excellent discipline of our schools is dowering the people of England with what Plato called the cosmetic art. The increasing refinement and gentility of our middle and lower classes cannot fail to encourage those who have laboured so long and so faithfully. But those who judge

by appearances often experience a painful disillusionment on coming to closer intimacy with
these men and women of good appearance, pleasing
manners, and real desire to do right, in finding
within such poverty of ideals, such crudity of
thought, such a lack of clear aim and high
purpose, belying all that their outward show
seemed to warrant. On the other hand, no one
can fail to have met men of humble origin, and
perhaps of uncouth appearance, who, with no
special advantages other than the possession of
a broad catholic faith, have been made gentle
by the inner refinement of their instincts and
thoughts, by a life lived in communion with
God. For, as Clement of Alexandria wrote, ' As
there is one mode of training for philosophers,
another for orators, and another for athletes, so
there is a generous disposition suitable to the
choice that is set upon moral loveliness resulting
from the training of Christ. And in the case of
those who have been trained according to this
influence, their gait in walking, their sitting at
table, their food, their sleep, their going to bed,
their regimen, and the rest of their mode of life,
acquire a superior dignity.' [1]

[1] *Paedagogus*, Book I, ch. xii, quoted in G. Hodgson's
Primitive Christian Education, p. 127. Cp. also J. R. Illing-
worth, *Christian Character* (Macmillan, 1904), ch. viii, p. 165 ;
R. C. Moberly, *Atonement and Personality* (Murray), fifth
edition, ch. x, p. 258 ; J. H. Newman, *The Idea of a University*,
Discourse VI, § 4.

III

The common ground.

What is wanted, therefore, in order to raise religious teaching out of amateurishness, and to place its powers at the service of education, is a scientific study of the department of Pastoral Theology which coincides with a part of the science of education, and a thorough investigation of the mutual relations of the one to the other in that area.

This must be prefaced by a history of religious education in the past, to see what has already been done and to learn by the success or the failure of others. Side by side with this the various existing undertakings and methods should be examined, their results discussed, and possible improvements suggested, by means of conferences or societies for informal discussion.

The theory of Christian education.

The whole theory of Christian education needs to be thought out and tested by the actual experience of facts. Then it requires to be clearly formulated and diligently propagated in its main broad outlines, as no system of education can be successfully carried out unless understood and approved of by the mass of the people. This higher conception needs to be preached against the crude ideas popularly current as to the purpose and value of schooling. At present these are almost entirely superficial and utilitarian, whether expressed in the common feminine criticism that ' With all this education I can't get a cook ', or in its masculine counterpart that ' My office boy doesn't know how to write an ordinary business letter '—which, apart from the false social theory involved, implies that the school ought to teach what can only be learned in the kitchen or in the office—up to the suggestion of the Poor Law Report that the teaching given to children in elementary schools should be more ' helpful to them in after-life '.[1] Certainly the aim of education is to fit a child to enter into life, but the Christian conception of life is not that of possession of an abundance of things ; it regards it as not depending on bread alone ; it holds that entrance to it is conditioned by keeping the Commandments ; that the attaining of all things that we need, all the wealth of culture and all the glory of the world, depends on seeking the kingdom of God and His righteousness first ; that it is not the aggressive and blatant, but the meek, that really inherit the earth.   This is based on the Christian view of man's nature, as having body, mind, and spirit, each needing balanced harmonious development by a training that will discipline the emotions, sanctify the intellect, and brace and strengthen the will.

The part played by worship in education of the feelings must be first considered.   The influence of the school chapel in boarding schools, the *The place of worship in education.*

[1] *Report of the Royal Commission on the Poor Laws and Relief of Distress*, vol. ii, part ix, section 128 (Wyman & Co., 1909).

custom of taking the children to church in day
schools whereby the same advantage is secured
for the son of the poor man, the relation of
week-day teaching to Sunday observance, the
connexion of institutional observances in orphan-
ages with normal church-going outside and in
after-life, all need to be studied. The question
of reaction if taking part in services is overdone must be weighed ; the crude statements
made by good people that their present lack of
religious practice is due to this cause need to be
put in their true light, for, in most cases, quite
obviously, it is in no way connected with it, and,
hardly less plainly, the strong healthy moral life,
which has survived the decay of their religion,
is due to just the teaching they deprecate. The
various questions of the frequency and length
of such services, of their nature and form, of the
place of music, of the style of preaching, of immediate edification, of preparation for after-life,
all need working out by the combined consideration of devout and observant teachers.

The sanctifi-
cation of the intellect.
So, again, with the sanctification of the intellect
and the preparation of the child's mind to find the
Christian interpretation of the world in after-life.
The actual methods of imparting religious knowledge need to be no less carefully considered. Here
much is being done and done well, especially on
the side of knowledge of the Bible and of Church
history. The chief need would seem to be that of

the direct application to doctrinal teaching of ordinary methods that have been tested and established in other subjects, and of a bringing of the whole body of dogma into closer relation to the facts of life.   This is largely a matter of text-books and time-tables.   The necessity of uncontroversial and dogmatic teaching for children, and the value of setting before students at universities, and in the sixth forms of schools, the varieties of opinions held in doctrinal matters, are both obvious ; the problem where one may leave off and the other begin, with all the practical consequences involved in school management, is one for experts to study.   Again, for all the questions of the training of the intellect a wide area of observation and experiment is needed.

In any Christian theory of education it would be agreed that morals are bound up with belief and religious practice, but clear ideas as to their relationships, and as to the best practical methods of building up character and educating the moral sense, are sorely needed.   Moral education as a system divorced from religion, or based upon reason alone, is, in the opinion of a Christian, bound to fail ; but mentally the moral aspect can be separated and studied with profit, while much can be learned from non-Christians who have its cause at heart.   The question how far it should be direct or implied, how far the former tends to create prigs or the latter to miss its mark, how far

Moral education.

self-examination is valuable or a danger, the age
at which, or the frequency with which, it should be
advised, the relative influence of religious practices,
religious lessons, and the tone of the school, the
value of understanding the reasons why things are
right or wrong, the power of forming clear and
rapid ethical judgements, the faculty of prompt
obedience to conscience, and the general training
of character, are all questions of this part of
religious education that need to be worked out.
The whole subject is to the fore at the present
time, and the Christian side needs to be presented
reasonably and with knowledge ; but this can only
be possible after much thought and long experience
on the part of practical men.[1]

IV

Co-oper-
ation.
The common ground of education and Pastoral
Theology needs to be studied. This can only be
effected by the co-operation of the living agents
in either science. The clergy and the teaching
profession need to come far more into contact with
one another as fellow workers in a common cause.
Did they meet more frequently in the class-room,

[1] Cp. *Moral Instruction and Training in Schools*, ed.
M. E. Sadler : vol. i, The United Kingdom ; vol. ii, Foreign
and Colonial (Longmans, 1908) ; *Papers on Moral Education*,
communicated to the first International Moral Education
Congress, held at the University of London, September 25-9,
1908 (David Nutt, 1908).

were they to meet formally, say each term, to discuss the various points of contact in their work, could conferences of those who have the matter at heart be arranged from time to time,[1] both Church and school would gain immensely.

[1] Cp. *Principles of Parish Work*, ch. vii, ' Young and Old.'

CHAPTER III

PASTORAL THEOLOGY AND SOCIOLOGY

RECENT years have witnessed a great advance in the study of Sociology from the Christian point of view, or, to use the phrase adopted by the Christian Social Union, ' in the light of the Incarnation.' That this has been of great profit, especially in the area of practical and philanthropic undertakings, need hardly be said. But there has been comparatively little reconsideration of Christianity itself in the light of modern sociological knowledge, though such a study would be of no less profit to religious work. Whether in the normal features of society as affecting Church life, in abnormal and pathological forms which offer obstacles to its progress, or in the more delicate questions of the mutual influence and general relationship of the two, the common grounds of Sociology and Pastoral Theology needs to be explored as part of a thorough treatment of the latter science.

I

Normal conditions of Society —the family. To begin with normal conditions : it is becoming more and more recognized that the family must be regarded as the unit of society ; but though the importance of the institution is often preached theoretically, the conception of the family itself is not clearly held and is often confused with that of the home. That latter conception, of which English people are so proud, is purely material ; it is comprised by the four walls of a house (with perhaps the addition of a garden) ; its chief rite is the Sunday dinner ; and it is no way inconsistent with a complete break-up of the family. This, indeed, often takes place within the home when husband and wife, elder sons and daughters, all work and regard themselves as units each paying his own way, while the children are taught, fed, and amused at school. The family, on the other hand, often survives the break-up of the home, possibly even becomes the stronger for it, and though its essential element and centre of force is the union of husband and wife, its influence extends to the third and fourth degree and to children's children.

But even when its real nature is clearly grasped, its existence is frequently ignored in practical Church work. Sunday schools have been established without any preliminary consideration of their probable effect on the conception of family duty.[1] For good or evil, we have effectually impressed on the mind of the working-class parent that it is his duty to send off his children to be taught by others, and not to take them to church himself. The work of clubs for men and boys, and

[1] Cp. *Principles of Parish Work*, p. 152, ' Sunday Schools.'

all the various schemes for ' getting hold of the lads ', are obviously doing much good ; but it is not so clear that, by ignoring the fact that husbands and sons are members of families, they are not incidentally doing much harm also. At any rate, they ought only to be started after a mature consideration of all the sociological questions incidentally involved. Again, the ' need of religion in the home ' is a phrase frequently employed not only by politicians, who regard it as necessitating its banishment from the school, but also by preachers and parish workers who, withal, are able to give very little practical advice as to how it should be fostered and taught. Obviously, what is now needed is the building up of a whole body of domestic pedagogy, similar to that which has been elaborated, at any rate in secular matters, for the school.[1]

Again, the still more difficult question of the natural dissolution of the family, as its younger members begin to prepare for the formation of independent centres of life, has been to a certain extent considered in the upbringing of the children of the better-educated classes, and a system of governesses, day schools, boarding schools, and universities has been established gradually to wean them from home and to accustom them to self-government and responsibility. But, even in our

[1] A beginning of this work has been made by the Mothers' Union. Cp. *Church Teaching at Home* (S.P.C.K.).

confirmation preparation it cannot be said that we have adequately solved the question of religious guidance through the ' awkward age ', or that we realize, for instance, the naturalness of the intense dislike of the family pew that often arises about the age of fifteen, and the harm that is done by insisting on its being occupied and offering no alternative form of worship.

There is a permanent contrast between the forms of social life in town and country. Possibly the distinction is not as great as we think, but in certain points it is marked. In the country it is impossible to ignore the structure of social life, for all its elements are visible day by day. In towns it is necessary to confine our direct acquaintance with its parts to one or two sections. This makes specialization of social study and action possible, and in turn benefits the country. There is constant action and reaction going on between the two. In matters ecclesiastical, the country is regularly supplying individuals to urban parishes, where it is possible to have finer churches and better music, to carry out ideals without opposition, and to form centres of learning. The obstructing or old-fashioned individuals who in village churches ' have to be considered ' can go elsewhere in the town. And, in turn, from the cathedrals and city churches flows back a stream of influence. Questions are fought out and customs established in the centres of

Town and country.

population, and the rural districts follow suit. The popular derivation of the word 'pagan' witnesses to this permanent feature in all propaganda.

But there is a corresponding danger of ignoring all but a section of society. No one can travel from one parish to another without becoming acutely conscious of the fact. Our methods of work in towns are largely country methods merely enlarged in area without being adapted, and it is unfortunately quite easy to fail to see their unsuitability and inefficiency so long as they deal more or less effectively with a section of the people. In our great cities there is always an extreme difficulty in grasping the social structure of the life round us owing to its far greater elaborateness and diffuseness. While in the country all the members of the family are known, and possibly all employed by the same person, in towns not only does each work in a different place, and for a different master, but professional and home life are lived in different spheres. The adaptation of parish work to these conditions is hard even to those who are in possession of a clear conception of the conditions, but most of us have not even a thought-out theory of social life.

Feudal and industrial conditions.

Moreover, the question has been complicated by the fact that the great increase in urban life is due to industrial causes, while country life is

still largely feudal. It is common to hear in-
dustrialism denounced and a radical change of
the structure of society demanded. But it is not
possible to say that it is wrong in itself, though
it may be in various unchristian developments ;
at any rate we have not at present sufficient
knowledge to condemn it altogether. Yet the
change that has been involved is as great as that
from the ancient civilization founded on slavery,
with problems such as St. Paul had to face, or
from the essentially military society of the later
Roman Empire that has left its stamp on the
Roman Church, to the feudal conditions of the
Middle Ages. A clear understanding of the nature
of the change involved would have immensely
aided the Church in her task of christianizing
the new forms of society as they arose, and the
historical study of sociological development will
be no less valuable in guiding us in present-day
problems.

Local differences of race probably have a great
influence in determining the form that religion
will take, especially in a mixed people like the
English. We are familiar with certain broad
distinctions, such as that between north and
south, or between the Celtic inhabitants of
western Cornwall and the Saxon stock to their
east. But there are probably slight but continuous influences at work in many parts where
Danish, Norse, or other elements preponderate,

Race differences.

about which we are, at present, quite in the dark.[1]

National variations. National and racial differences are more obvious, but it is chiefly in their superficial phenomena that they are noticed. The more scientific sociology of modern times seeks to trace the varieties of spirit from which they develop, and to find the causes of those varieties in natural features, to note the influence of valley and mountain, to mark the effect of climate or fertility of soil in forming character by the consequent ease or difficulty of living. So far as the deductions it makes are sound, there are obvious parallel questions waiting to be worked out in the sphere of religion.[2] The

[1] Cp. the following extract from a private letter : ' Experience has shown me that organization well fitted to a superior class of working man may be beyond the power of another to respond to, e. g. the H—— working classes (manufacturing, and Danish blood) are fifty years in advance of the W—— working classes (mining, and Angle or Mercian blood). The former demand, and respond to, work on co-operative lines ; the latter want authoritative leadership, and do not understand why you should work by committees. If you try the latter they disagree among themselves and are constantly trying to go back on past resolutions. I think some method of diagnosing the responsive powers of a parish is necessary to a complete Science of Pastoral Theology, i.e. that we should differentiate between different communities (Saxon, Celtic, Anglian, and Danish, &c., the stage of civilization and education they have been brought to by their work and other influences) as well as between the classes, sexes, and ages of our various parishioners.'

[2] An excellent example of the study of such a question may be found in J. Wilbois' *L'Avenir de l'Église Russe* (Bloud et Cie, Paris, 1907).

influence of Latin civilization in determining the
form Christianity shall take in the countries that
have come under its influence; the question
whether the lesser vigour of the Roman Catholic
races (if they are less vigorous) is due to their
religion, or the form of their religion to their
greater docility, or, maybe, to their different
estimate of the scale of virtues by which success
does not rank so high as among some schools of
Protestantism, are all familiar subjects of discussion. But included in these broad issues are
a number of minor details of practical administration in which means must be adapted to circumstances. The limits of national variation and
the extent of ground common to all nations; the
point at which national instinct resents uniformity,
and when to urge it, involves a loss of touch
with people,—all such questions need working out
practically and inductively on a basis of sociological science.

But out of all this one thing emerges with
clearness and certainty, that merely individual or
' personal ' work is useless, or nearly so, if only
from the size of the field. For a small cottage
garden there is nothing like spade work, and this
method of agriculture still persists among the back-
ward races of the East. But for modern industrial
life the vast farms of the Far West are a necessity,
with their heavy labour lightened by machinery
directed by the intelligence of man, and in

' Per-
sonal
work.'

spiritual fields 'white for the harvest' there is
the same need of co-operation and organization
to gather the wheat into the barn.[1]   But further,
man is, as Aristotle said, by nature a citizen.
He is what he is in his relationships, and is a part
of all that he has met. If he disregards this and
tries, like Peer Gynt, to 'be himself', he passes
through selfishness to its conclusion in madness ;
if it is ignored by those who try to help him, he is
not understood and the help fails. In trying to deal
with individuals apart from their social relationships we deceive ourselves in every direction. We
make unconscious selections and judge whole
classes by them. We are taken in by externals,
by voice, by manner, by mood, by dress. Moreover, the single man so taken out of his setting acts
up to the words and expectations of the person
who is speaking to him. We are only able to
get at the outside of a man of another class if he
is taken for the time out of that class ; what we
say or do is quite external to his life, and has little
influence on it. We do not 'know' such people ;
for to get knowledge we must share some common
ground. It is only by working with people (except
in the case of natural relationships) that we can
really know them. The disappointment that comes

[1] The following advertisement appeared in a Church
paper on March 3, 1911 : 'Title offered—7000 people—Good
experience and training—Visiting prime essential—*Spade
husbandry*.'

from disregarding this fact of Sociology is familiar to all Church workers, but its cause is not generally grasped. The result is that a vast amount of Church work—visiting to 'get to know your people', social gatherings, &c.—is based on a false idea, and is recommended and urged in a way that would be impossible to any one with a more adequate conception of society.

II

The study of Sociology is more popularly associated with questions of abnormal conditions of society; to the majority of men it gains its interest from its connexion with poverty and the relief of distress. By the former is generally meant the more permanent inequalities of our social structure, and by the latter exceptional difficulties, arising often from unforeseen circumstances; but in either case it is an abnormal state with which we have to deal. *Abnormal conditions of society.*

This is not to say that naturally all men should be alike. There will, fortunately, always be differences in individuals, whether of temperament, character, or ability, and these differences will tend to work out in modifications of the social position of each. Besides this, there is, in all but the lowest and simplest forms of civilization, need for division of labour and for different people to do different kinds of work. The problem who is to do the dirty work has always been one of the *Varieties and inequalities.*

great difficulties in devising Utopias. But the aim of an ideal Commonwealth is not to secure equality in the sense of uniformity, but to make it possible for each to become perfect in his sphere. This implies the greatest differentiation possible so that each may be able to meet the other (if he desires it) on the common ground of efficiency, whether his own work be with head or hand. This will cure social inequalities socially, by raising class ideals rather than by raising individuals out of their class.

But Christ never disguised the real nature of poverty. ' He called want " want ", and evil He called " evil ".' [1] The wrong lies not in the existence of class differences, but in stereotyping bad conditions connected with them, or in hardening them into castes. There must be equality of opportunity for all, so that each can do his duty and realize himself in that state of life unto which it shall please God to call him. But it must be

[1] A. Harnack, *Das Wesen des Christentums* (1900), Lecture VI, p. 60 : ' Die Behauptung, Jesus habe eine allgemeine Verarmung und Verelendung so zu sagen gewünscht, um dann über diesen miserablen Zustand sein Himmelreich heraufzuführen—eine Behauptung, der man in verschiedenen Wendungen begegnet—ist falsch. Das Gegenteil ist richtig. Er hat Not Not und Uebel Uebel genannt.' (The idea that Jesus desired a universal diffusion of poverty and misery, and the establishment of His kingdom on this condition of wretchedness—an idea that we find in many directions—is false. The opposite is the truth. He called want ' want ', and evil He called ' evil '.)

God that calls him, and not man who fixes him there by arbitrary decisions. It is true that in material and spiritual things to him that hath shall be given, but just for that reason it is man's business to see that among his fellows there is none that hath not. This must be acknowledged if men of different stations are to be served. Any action that fails to allow for differences, and any that tends to stereotype them by assuming that abnormal states are permanent and inevitable, must be wrong.

The first thing, therefore, is to recognize that social inequalities exist, and so to construct our work that all needs may be met. This is already roughly attempted, but our methods need much more careful consideration. Mothers' Meetings, Working Men's Clubs, Sunday Schools, &c., are intended only for one class. In the present state of things they may be valuable ; as permanent institutions they are fatal. People talk of parishes where ' there is hardly anything to do as there are no poor ' ; often such places are in reality strong, active, and busy centres of religious life, but the phrase, besides being untrue, shows a serious misapprehension of the duty of the Church. Missions are held for ' the poor ', but no one ever heard of a ' mission to the lower middle class ', or ' to people who only keep one servant '. Yet the first expression is every bit as offensive as the two latter would be. On the other hand, so long

Differences to be recognized.

as some are less educated than others, preaching must obviously be adapted to different congregations. While some people have to do without help in their housework, hours of service must be suited to their needs.[1] Identical habits may even take very different forms under different conditions ; thus a men's afternoon service consisting mainly of an address, which seems to meet a real need among artisans, has possibly its exact counterpart, *mutatis mutandis*, in the University Sermon following an earlier Chapel service.[2]

But beyond such more obvious matters there is a host of other questions which must affect pastoral work. The ways in which different classes get their ideas ; the relative influence of the Press, conversation, and tradition ; the proportion in which the appeal to the intellect or the feelings meets with a response, a matter of obvious importance in mission work in which preaching and argument at present play so large a part ; the opinions which, rightly or wrongly, men hold as to methods of Church work—as, for instance, that of the ordinary Anglo-Indian on Christian Missions, or of artisans on the clergy visiting their wives while they are at work—however biased or ignorant these may be in themselves ; the concep-

---

[1] Roughly we provide services at 11 a.m. for those with, and at 7 p.m. for those without, servants ; but this hardly meets the problem adequately.

[2] Cp. *Principles of Parish Work*, ch. vi, ' Rich and Poor.'

tion of religion and morals, and the modes of religious expression natural to the uneducated; their use of words; the pace at which they can read or sing in a service without losing the thread of meaning in what is said—all influence the methods adopted, and need, therefore, to be studied on the basis of a far more delicate and accurate sociology.

To disregard them involves an immense waste of moral force. Conventional opinions, such as that 'the poor are nicer than the middle classes', or the assumption, based, it would seem, on a study of the literature of tracts, that they are more pious, will go uncorrected. It is only too easy to mix with people of another class and to see absolutely nothing of their lives, to be in external contact with their doings and to be quite out of touch with their real selves. J. S. Mill in his autobiography declared that 'a person of high intellect should never go into unintellectual society unless he can enter it as an apostle', as those who do so are 'almost without exception greatly deteriorated by it'. It is necessary for a missionary to put himself in an unnatural social position if he is to do good, and risk deterioration if need be; but to be in such a position does no good in itself, though the mere fact of its unnaturalness makes us feel as if it did. It may be a mere act of patronage, or be due to that strange attraction that intercourse with inferiors often

Danger of ignoring class differences.

presents, with its sense of ease, of freedom from responsibility, of intellectual superiority, of licence to make statements without fear of their being challenged. It may be right to mix familiarly with uneducated boys, or a duty to live in continual companionship with middle-class ideas, but, if so, it is done at a risk which is run for greater ends. It should be carefully considered, on the other hand, whether the violent dislocating of individuals from their normal surroundings for a day or two into conditions they cannot understand is a desirable thing, as when working-class lads are plunged for a bank holiday into what appears to them the waste and idleness of University life. It may be that a far greater result would be obtained, even for the same class, by social intercourse with those who are nearer in mind and are themselves in some way leaders of men (as, for instance, of school managers with teachers), than by means of many of the social experiments now carried on. The great value of the Settlement idea is that the work done is social and not individual, and that the residents take part in the normal life of the neighbourhood.

Influence of class ideals.

The failure to realize the existence of classes and the influence of their ideals may be traced in other ways, and is all the more serious because where this influence is present it acts subtly and continuously. The consequence of our general custom of entrusting the rendering of a large part of our services to uneducated choir boys is probably enormous in the aggregate, and must seriously lower the type and conception of public worship. A number of little things done by vergers and caretakers drawn from the same class, whose idea of a church is a place to be kept locked except when it must be opened, instead of being one to be kept open except when it must be shut up, probably oppose to the growth of the spirit of devotion a serious obstacle which, even when recognized, it is difficult to remove. On the other hand, the unconscious influence of an organist of a cultured mind and devout spirit is even more powerful, and the piety that a Christian architect may have built into a church is a permanent help to religion.

The danger of a class ministry is one of which we in England have had experience, but it will not be avoided by substituting another of an inferior class. There are men, no doubt, with a vocation to the priesthood in all classes, but those who start with no social advantages need for that very reason a longer and more careful preparation. The priest should be of no class, or rather of all classes, but in the present inequality of conditions that is impossible. He must aim at being able to mix with all if he is to preach to and to influence them, but first of all as a necessary preliminary he must set himself to study, understand, and work with, those of other grades.

III

The relation of Church and social life.

Behind all the questions of the normal and abnormal elements of society which we have been considering in their influence on Pastoral Theology, lies the greater one of the whole mutual relationship of social and religious organizations and institutions. Their area is often the same, and the matter they deal with identical. Certain acts belong to one and certain to the other, but often it is difficult to draw the dividing line. Sometimes a single act serves two different purposes ; thus in the country a visit alike in all externals may be paid in a social or in a pastoral capacity without the two aims being separated. In towns it is less difficult to differentiate social and parochial life, but the identification of the two causes more practical confusion. The close identification of social and pastoral actions may in certain cases be right, but if right it should be made consciously.

Certain activities are connected with pastoral work though essentially they are different. It will always remain a part of Christian duty to exercise charity, but the administration of alms is in itself no part of Pastoral Theology, though at the present moment such social work bids fair to crush out all opportunity even for the consideration of more important matters. A clergyman has his duty both as a man and a citizen, but his work as such should not take up the time and energy claimed by his special duties.   On the other hand, the consideration of the moral effect of bad administration of charity, of the consequences to religion of allowing profession of religion to be associated with relief in the minds of the uneducated, and the carrying out of practical measures for preventing, or reforming, these evils, are certainly part of his business.

It is recognized that the Church should stand apart from party politics, and in England, at any rate, she only departs from this principle when attacked by a party, and reluctantly even then. But the best method of securing this independence has not been worked out in practice ; and the rival views—on the one hand, that the Church should rather let herself be wronged than take part in public affairs ; and on the other, that she should form a policy on purely ecclesiastical questions, with an organization to insist on its being carried out—have not been threshed out to any conclusion. *Politics.*

Similar questions are those connected with Disestablishment,[1] which are much more far-reaching than men realize.   Beyond the mere political issue of the advantage or disadvantage to the country, the effect on the Church of association with the State in all the varying degrees from mutually independent co-operation (such as exists *Church and State.*

[1] I need not say that I use the word in its natural sense, and not as a euphemism for disendowment.

in Scotland in the case of the Established Kirk) up to the extreme of Erastianism, needs to be considered scientifically on a basis of observed and tested fact. The weakening of the relationship has gone on in the last generation almost un-observed ; and the consequence to the Church needs an unbiased examination to see whether the connexion hampers and secularizes her, or whether it is a source of strength. In regard to its effect on the nation, we have to consider whether it is better to assume that the State is Christian, and so commit it to certain principles, or whether it is better to accept the fact that Christians are a remnant, and can work more effectively from outside.[1] Further questions are— the consequences of either policy at home to-day ; and the better course for to-morrow in the mission-field as the proportion of Christians to the whole population grows. In short, the problems of the fourth century all need thinking out over again. The rival claims of Caesar and God do not clash ' so long as Caesar's self be God's ' ;[2] but when

---

[1] Cp. W. Hobhouse, Bampton Lectures, *The Church and the World in Idea and History*.

[2] Crashaw, *Steps to the Temple*, Divine Epigrams, Mark xii :

> Give to Caesar——
> Give to God——
> All we have is God's, and yet
> Caesar challenges a debt ;
> Nor hath God a thinner share,
> Whatever Caesar's payments are ;

the phrase ' we have no king but Caesar ' implies that he is merely the reflex of the opinion of the natural man, and the tendency becomes predominant to accept his authority as final in matters of the marriage law, of education, and of the whole moral standard, then it is necessary to have a clear understanding of the duties of man to the two kingdoms of which he is a member.

The Church has to adapt her methods to all conditions of human society unless they can definitely be proved incompatible with her faith. To certain changes she has already accommodated herself. Thus, the discovery of printing has greatly modified our lives ; and in the use of books of common and private prayer, or in the development of hymnody, full advantage has been taken of the opportunity presented, though in the popular use of the Press the English Church has been less active than other religious bodies. Again, the invention of gas and electric light have brought about certain marked changes in social customs ; and in the development of evening services the Church has shown herself flexible in meeting new conditions. Easier means of locomotion have broken down the old local bonds ; and as society is slowly reconstructing itself under new

Changing social customs.

> All is God's ; and yet, 'tis true,
> All we have is Caesar's too.
> All is Caesar's ; and what odds,
> So long as Caesar's self is God's ?

conditions, the Church is following suit though still sadly hampered by parochialism. The growing custom in large towns of 'week-ending' is probably due to a natural need for more relaxation and change in view of the increasing strain and intensity of life ; if so, it is useless to declaim against it or to deplore the fact that it decimates congregations ; the Church must show herself sufficiently fertile in evolving new methods to provide for the religious needs of people in new circumstances which she has no right to condemn. The great growth of hotel life, with its lack of local duties and social responsibilities, and the conditions of life that it creates for an army of employees, is a development less easily justified. Whether, however, it be natural or abnormal, it is equally useless to declaim. The task of the Church is to do her best to serve the spiritual needs of the people involved, but this can only be done after first studying and understanding the social complications that have occurred.

Danger of specialization.
The obvious advantages of specializing work in this way are those that come from thoroughness and concentration of effort. But there is also a danger of not being aware of the existence of other classes which may lead to serious consequences. The general absence of the artisan classes from public worship is acknowledged as a fact, but is not, as a rule, realized till, say, the need of finding a new sexton reveals the smallness

of the field of choice, or the report of the presence of thirty thousand men at a football match on Christmas morning gives a graphic illustration of the materialism of the manual worker. Even in the social strata where the Church is alive and often powerful, there are whole groups and classes who are hardly conscious of her existence, as witness the clumsy blunders of politicians, or the moral ideas and presuppositions of novelists. The loss to art, politics, and literature, from the inadequacy of the Church to cope with a highly complex society is incalculable.

The Church, again, in many of her functions, is bound up with the commercial ties of society. All that is involved in this fact also needs working out, for various questions of finance and government arise in the parish and in diocesan work. In certain of these, as, for instance, in account-keeping, she must obviously conform to the recognized standards of business. In others, such as in questions of government, of committees, of representation, the forms of procedure, of minute-keeping, of letter-filing, &c., should perhaps be identical, and the questions of the basis of franchise, the limitations of popular power, though fundamentally different, may still be analogous ; but both the similarity and the difference need careful thinking out. *Commercial sociology.*

How far the Church should link herself to the social structure of her surroundings it is difficult to decide, but that a close connexion exists at present is obvious. No one can visit many churches, especially in country districts, without becoming aware of the way in which the two are interwoven, how largely churchgoing has its roots in the social order. Even in towns people who have no other religious practice come to church for funerals and weddings, showing how strong is the association in that it lingers long after other customs have dropped off. This has a great value as a conservative force, and, no doubt, carries many a man over times of doubt and indifference, but there is an equally great danger in relying on it. This danger is seen most clearly in urban parishes where methods based on the identification of the Church with one particular social order have proved so ineffective because circumstances have changed and the social structure is in dissolution.

Spirit-
ual
socio-
logy.

We need, besides, an independent and purely spiritual sociology of the Church, for ' we are, each one, citizens of one true city ',[1] and live as

---

[1] Cp. Dante, *Purg.* xiii. 94 :

> ' . . . ciascuna è cittadina
> D' una vera città ; ma tu vuoi dire
> Che vivesse in Italia peregrina.'
> (We are each one citizens
> Of one true city. Any, thou wouldst say,
> Who lived a pilgrim in Italia's land.)

Aug. in Ps. cxviii : ' Qui vero cives sunt in populo Dei, ipsi sunt in terra peregrini.' (But they who are citizens among the people of God are pilgrims on earth.)

pilgrims on earth. This is to be created by the same methods that have done so much for the understanding of secular society, by observation and comparison, by patient investigation and humble submission to facts. But this is not so much a question of the relationship between Sociology and Pastoral Theology as a part of the study of the pure science of the latter.

CHAPTER IV

THE MATERIAL OF PASTORAL THEOLOGY

The aim of classification.
IN classifying the subject-matter of Pastoral Theology our aim is threefold. We want to get an idea of the whole area and scope of the science, to secure a sense of proportion in the different parts, and to facilitate specialization in the various departments. We have to see what has already been worked out and what remains to be done ; as a master in a school draws up a time-table to ensure a well-balanced building up of the child's mind and character, so we want to map out the different branches of study without laying undue stress on any one to the neglect of others ; and as in a library there are special departments for manuscripts, books, periodical publications, newspapers, and catalogues, to meet the needs of various classes of students, so we want to mark out the different sources to which students may turn for facts on which to base the working out of any single point.[1]

[1] A similar work has already been done for Theology itself, which has been well systematized. Students at the Universities aim at getting a general knowledge of the whole field under the four general headings of (1) Biblical Theology, including the study of Hebrew and Hellenistic Greek, N.T. exegesis, textual

I

In the majority of works on the subject there is a certain arrangement of the matter based on practical experience.   It is true that some English books published in connexion with endowed lectures on Pastoral Theology frankly abandon the subject altogether, and deal with purely theological matters with, perhaps, some special reference to the clergy.   Others merely relate personal experiences.   Most are simply reprinted lectures.   Where they deal with special subjects they are often admirable,[1] but even then they are seldom written with a consciousness that they are contributions to a larger whole, or with the intention of filling up gaps in a complete system.   Such works, excellent as many are, do little towards building up a science, while their tendency is to stereotype defects by encouraging the development of subjects which already occupy sufficient

Empirical classification.

and higher criticism ;   (2) Dogmatic Theology, including Dogmatics, Moral Theology, and special aspects of Philosophy and Psychology ;   (3) Ecclesiastical History, including that of Doctrine, of the Canon, and of the Church ;   and (4) Applied Theology, including Liturgiology, Apologetics, and what is loosely termed ' Pastoralia '.   This latter division practically covers the same area as what we have called the pure science of Pastoral Theology.   Afterwards post-graduate students specialize in any one or more of these departments.

[1] e.g. *The Cure of Souls,* by W. Cunningham, D.D., F.B.A. (Cambridge University Press, 1908), dealing with the history of the position of the English clergyman.

attention. Just as a person practising a piece of music on the piano without a teacher tends to go over the parts which he already knows and to shirk the difficult passages, so a vast number deal only with the threadbare topic of preaching, and deal with it badly because in isolation from the rest.[1]

Still, there may be noticed a general tendency to divide the subject into three parts : Liturgiology, preaching and teaching, and ' practical work '. This is, perhaps, specially noticeable in German Lutheran works, which are often models of method and at times revel in technical terms, *Liturgik, Homiletik, Katechetik, Poimenik*—we find even such words as *Keryktik, Koinonik,* and *Kybernetik*—but do not for all this always escape the onesidedness that we wish to avoid. For these divisions have grown up largely by chance from unscientific work. They have merely systematized what is already there, in a field which to English Churchmen seems a very narrow one. Now systematization, though necessary for science, is not science in itself.[2] To make work scientific we need, as we saw, a clear understanding of the nature of scientific method, an understanding

---

[1] The German Lutheran and Protestant Nonconformist works alluded to in Book I, ch. iii, are perhaps the greatest failures in this respect.

[2] Cp. P. Drews, *Das Problem der praktischen Theologie* (Mohr, Tübingen, 1910), pp. 20 ff., for some admirable criticism of over-systematization.

exercised by the analogy of other sciences, and based on a wide conception of the matter in hand—in this case of the nature of the Church and of the calling of the clergy. Science seeks for laws and principles ; can we find these underlying this empirical classification ? If so it may stand for the present, while we reconstruct the whole more thoroughly and profoundly.

What are the chief intrinsic elements of Pastoral Theology ? To discern these we must go back to our definition on page 36. Pastoral Theology is the science of the work of man in helping his fellow man in his relationships to God. This involves three main elements based on the study of man in relation to God, of God as apprehended by man, of man in relation to his fellow man under God.   *Three main divisions of Pastoral Theology.*

Man must be studied in his relationships to God before his fellow man can help him in them. This must be done on a basis of sound Psychology. Man, so long as he is on earth, bears about him his limitations,[1] and must approach God under them. Hence the necessity of sacraments and forms. God is not bound by them, but we are. He expects men to express themselves in human language even   *Devotion.*

---

[1] ' Et laudare te vult homo, aliqua portio creaturae tuae ; et homo circumferens mortalitatem suam, circumferens testimonium peccati sui, et testimonium quia superbis resistis : et tamen laudare te vult homo, aliqua portio creaturae tuae,' Aug. *Conf.* i. 1.

while they know that it is imperfect. This necessity involves a whole range of phenomena of religious expression based on underlying human laws of worship and inner life. These may be either social or individual. They can be grouped under the three titles of Liturgiology, which deals with common prayer; of Ascetic theology, which treats of individual human spiritual discipline; and of Christian Art, which embodies both of these in material forms. In short, under this head may be grouped all that we saw to be connected with the work of a clergyman as Minister of the Eucharist.

Evange-
lization.

God is apprehended by man also through his understanding. The conditions and limitations under which this takes place must be studied on a basis of educational and metaphysical science. That is, the laws of evangelization and of apprehension of truth must be searched for, the truth itself studied, and its propaganda considered. Such matter can be ranged under the titles of Dogmatics, the study of the tenets of a living body (which are therefore bound up with practical consequences) as distinct from that of the history of doctrine ; of Exegesis, the interpretation of Scripture as a basis of authority ; of Homiletics, the art of preaching to confirm or to convert ; of Catechetics, the science of educating the ignorant ; of Apologetics, the art of defending Christianity ; and of Mission lore, that deals with the extension of the domain of the Church. Under this second head may be gathered all that we saw was involved in the clergyman's duties as Evangelical and Minister of the Word.

Finally man has a special relation to man and God together. This must be looked for reverently on a basis of sociological experience. To do so will lead us on to the whole science of Ethics, and to all that is vaguely called 'practical work'. Among its departments are those of Casuistry, which seeks for guidance in individual cases of conscience, of Canon Law, which governs the polity of the Church as a whole, of principles of management in the parish and of moral education in the school, of the philanthropy that is known as 'Church work', of larger matters of social duty. All this is concerned with the activities demanded from the clergy as Ministers of Baptism. *Practical duty.*

This arrangement, then, though adopted instinctively and on empirical grounds, is based on the fundamental conceptions of Pastoral Theology ; it is in agreement with the nature of man as body, mind, and will ; it harmonizes with practical experience and with the conception of the duties of the clergy considered in Book II, ch. i ;[1] and it fits in with our consideration of the allied *This classification scientific.*

---

[1] Though, as we are no longer considering the question of the training of the clergy, the order of those duties has been recast. There we followed the order suggested by practical work, and began with the conception of the clergyman as Minister of Baptism, while here we have taken the logical order following the conception of man as body, mind, and will.

sciences which, as we found, need to be examined
first.   So far as classification of the subject-matter
goes we may fairly claim to have placed our work
on a scientific basis.

II

Two
methods
of study.
It is not enough, however, to know the kind of
matter to look for : we must also have some idea
where to find it.   The data of our science may
be divided into two great masses, according as
we discover them in the past or in the present.
They are made up of impressions drawn partly
from a world of which only records remain, and
partly from observation and experience in the
living world around.

Histori-
cal—in
the facts
of the
past.
Pastoral Theology, that is, may first be studied
historically.   This is not the same as studying the
history of Pastoral Theology.   As we saw above,
there is very little history of the science itself,
but the historical field from which we can gather
material is vast and reaches far back into the
distance.   It may be studied in the phenomena
of worship in the past, in ritual customs, in the
growth and spread of popular devotions, in the
evolution of ideas of priesthood and sacrifice and
all that is involved in them.   We may note forms
of the intellectual expression of religion in tracing
the history of doctrine, of apologetics, or of
preaching.   We may look for the record of practical conceptions of Christian duty as revealed in

Canon Law, in the evolution of moral standards, in the development of casuistry, in the growth of missions. The first may be found in liturgies, in archaeological remains, in churches, in prayer books, in traditional customs, or in folk-lore. Varying forms of religious thought have left their traces in sermons, in catechisms, and in creeds. Successes or failures in pastoral work have been chronicled in biographies, in stories of missions, in parish histories and records. From these we can draw evidence as to various movements of spiritual life, thought, or experiment, which will enable us to trace their origin and development, and to test their permanence and value. But these studies must always be ' pastoralized ', that is, they must be studied with a view of throwing light on modern parallels, since the history of the past interprets the present and prophesies the future.[1]

As an example we may take the custom of public prayer twice a day. This may be illustrated by Jewish and other primitive customs.[2] In the early Church it reappears as the popular form.[3]

e. g. of prayer twice a day.

[1] Cp. Aug. *De Doct. Christ.*, Book III, ch. x: ' Praeteritorum narratio est futurorum praenuntiatio, praesentium demonstratio.' (The story of the past is the foretelling of the future, the explanation of the present.)

[2] Dom S. Bäumer, *Histoire du Bréviaire*, vol. i, ch. i, p. 56 note, p. 185.

[3] Aug. *Conf.*, Book V, ch. ix ; Bingham, *Antiquities*, XIII, ix. 8 ; W. C. Bishop, ' The Mozarabic Breviary,' *Church Quarterly Review*, April 1911.

Attempts to increase the number of services were only partly successful among a small body of ascetics. Similar endeavours by monastic bodies were made in obedience to theories, but in practice the numerous offices tended to be grouped together in two main agglomerations. This tendency reasserted itself in the private use of the breviary when Latin ceased to be a spoken language and the choir offices could no longer be popular services. It was boldly acted upon by Cranmer in recasting the English Daily Office, and with success.[1] We have here evidence of a permanent instinct in human nature involving liturgical consequences which are of the utmost practical importance to-day.

In the opinions of men —past and present.

Or we may study Pastoral Theology from the opinions of men, as they have from time to time reflected on their religious practices and have formulated theories of them. These may be found in the records of history, or heard in every-day conversation. Some have been elaborated, threshed out, perhaps discredited after patient examination ; others are being formed in the daily clash of thought with thought. Men have pondered on the conceptions underlying tradi-tional worship and ritual ; they have elaborated

[1] ' The custom of praying seven times a day has long since ceased, and we now assemble only twice a day for prayers.' Cranmer's second scheme for reform of the Breviary, Gasquet and Bishop, *Edward VI and the Book of Common Prayer*, pp. 31, 376.

liturgical principles, given mystical interpretations
to religious acts, and created a whole language of
conscious symbolism.[1]   In the present day they
are discussing the meaning and purpose of
ceremonial, and might with profit be tracing the
relation of church architecture to the needs of
public worship, or examining the psychology of
pilgrimages, pageants, and revivals.   The question
of the connexion of creed and character, the
difference of doctrine and dogma—of religious
truth, that is, studied for itself, and in its bearing
on the ideals and actions of a religious body—
the Christian interpretation of the world, the laws
of rhetoric, the art of apologetic, are all matters
which refer to the intellect of men in its religious
aspect.   Again, the philosophy of Christian practice, the growth of ecclesiastical discipline and
of casuistry, the nature of penitence, the use of
punishments, suggest directions in which Pastoral
Theology has much to learn.

The data for these inquiries will be found in
liturgical treatises and in philosophical works,
in books on Pastoral Theology as an independent
study, and in ' parsons' handbooks ' of all descrip-
tions.   The opinions and reflections of men—or

---

[1] Cp. W. H. Frere, *The Principles of Religious Ceremonial*,
'The Oxford Library of Practical Theology' (Longmans, 1906) ;
The Ornaments of the Church, Report of Sub-Committee of
Upper House of Convocation of Canterbury, No. 416 (1908),
p. 33.

sometimes the opinions formed without reflecting
—which contribute to our material must be
sought in popular agitations (as distinct from
unconscious movements) and controversies in the
past, or in their counterparts of to-day as recorded
in the Press, in articles and correspondence,[1] in
novels, in debates, in conversations. These have
to be tested for their soundness and their significance ; they must be weighed and marshalled to
judge their importance ; they must, above all, be
checked by facts.

e.g.
Chris-
tian
apologe-
tic.
As an example we may take the question of
the place and value of Christian apologetic. This
may be traced from its beginning in the second
century when it was forced on an unprepared
Church by persecution. The effectiveness of the
defence should be gauged, and note taken as to
what told. The impressiveness of an elaborate
scheme of constructive theology as a defence may
be examined in Augustine's *De Civitate Dei*, in the
Summa of Thomas Aquinas, in Butler's *Analogy*,
and their effect in their own times and in later days
estimated. Again, the rules of debate may be
studied theoretically in books, in Aristotle, Cicero,
Quintilian, Longinus ; or in more modern works

---

[1] Such as *Do We Believe ?* with an Introduction by W. L.
Courtney, M.A., LL.D. (Hodder & Stoughton, 1905), a reprint
of letters published in the *Daily Telegraph* ; or *Les Divorcés
peints par eux-mêmes*, Mille et une Confessions recueillies par
Gustave Téry (Paris, Arthème Fayard).

such as Whately's *Rhetoric*, and the numerous handbooks for speakers ; or as a living art in newspaper controversies, in public meetings, at street corners, in the mission-field. If this were done there is little doubt that much less time and nervous force would be wasted, and far more people made to understand the real nature of the Christian creed.

Or, again, Pastoral Theology may be studied experimentally, in the present and from direct observation. If this method is adopted, the student will concentrate his attention on the phenomena of present-day religious life. He will study the features of various religious bodies to note their differences and their common ground ; he will mark the vigour and growth of customs ; he will analyse the interest in details of ceremonial that seems so trivial ; he will try experiments in church arrangements, and keep his eyes open to see if they help or hinder devotion ; he will consider questions of church-planning in their practical relation to the uses to which the buildings are to be put (a point so strangely neglected by many architects) ; he will try to gauge the effect and value of new forms of services, and will aim at getting a fine perception as to what stimulates, and what weakens, religious life.

As regards living opinions, he will watch to see how they are spread ; he will study methods of teaching as they are actually practised in schools ;

The facts of the present.

he will observe cautiously the phenomena of conversion ; he will set himself to learn from experts the lessons of mission work, and will search for analogies to home work in experience gained abroad ; he will consider the efficacy of present-day preaching, and watch to discover instruments for a new evangelism. In 'practical work' he will study the various methods adopted for parish management and organization, as well as for dealing with individuals ; he will note critically the real effect of clubs and visiting ; he will study, that is, the whole work being done and to be done.

The field in which the subject-matter will be found for this is the whole world around us, but especially the men and women in the Church itself, and the various institutions and undertakings which they conduct. It will be noticed that in this case it will necessarily rather be width of observation that is possible, while the historical method supplied the test of permanence in time. There is no fear of unreality or lack of vividness in this direct way of study ; the danger is rather that of hastiness or inaccuracy. There will, therefore, be all the more need of care in observation, of accurate noticing of facts, and of diligent collecting of evidence.

Corresponding to the two classes of student.

These questions of method in the actual constructive work of Pastoral Theology will occupy our attention in the next section ; but, before we pass on, we must notice that these two broad divisions of historical and direct methods, of abstract and experimental science, correspond to the two classes of student which as we saw in Book II, ch. iii, would be produced by training. In specializing, each must work with a consciousness of what the other is doing. The historian and the philosopher must study Pastoral Theology in the past, but with constant reference to present needs ; the practical man must be careful to observe all things in the light of the past. So alone shall we get both the breadth and the directness needed for scientific work.

BOOK IV

THE METHOD OF PASTORAL THEOLOGY

' In matters which concern the actions of God, the most dutiful way on our part is to search what God hath done, and with meekness to admire that, rather than to dispute what He in congruity of reason ought to do.'—HOOKER, *Ecclesiastical Polity*, Book III, xi. 21.

CHAPTER I

THE FACULTY OF OBSERVATION

WE have examined the method of the science, and have considered both the training of the student and the material he is to work with ; we have now to see how he is to apply the method to the matter.

I

Observation of data.
At the outset we are struck with its enormous mass and variety, for by our definition it consists of the numberless outward expressions of all that concerns man's work in the relationships of his fellow man to God. We are to observe all that can be known of the opinions, judgements, and feelings of men in matters of religion, to look for

them in records oral and written, in conversations, in official utterances, in private confidences, in correspondence, in biographies, in novels, in the daily Press. We are to study how the religion of men works itself out in visible sacramental forms with which others can have contact, in rites, in organizations, in orders of ministry, in permanent institutions, in practical experiments. These grow more varied in their phenomena also as they develop in all classes of society, at different ages, among the various races of mankind, while, besides the great accumulation that is revealed in the ordinary course of religious life, there are all the abnormal and pathological symptoms of those who are sick in soul.

Moreover, in many cases the task is one of the utmost delicacy. Often we are dealing with what is the most sacred in the inner lives of men. Experiment, except within limits soon reached, is dangerous. As in the study of Psychology the possibility of a science has often been contested, so here many would deny that we can make such careful observations as will give us data enough for scientific study. On the other hand, the delicacy of the work is compensated for by its directness. Pastoral Theology shares with physical science an advantage that it has over that of history in that the things looked for are for the most part living and seen by direct observation. Many of them are drawn from immediate personal

Difficult but direct.

experience, and in all there is the stimulus of an intense and vivid interest.[1]

Powers of observation are largely acquired, as we learned in our youth when we read the story of *Eyes and No-eyes*, while Mr. Sherlock Holmes and the Boy Scout movement have impressed the fact on the popular mind. Good scouting is the basis of tactics, and it must be accurate, complete, sharp, and imaginative.

Accuracy of vision.

Accuracy of observation is the first requisite. Many persons appear to be constitutionally unable to see things exactly, or, indeed, in some cases, to see anything at all. They are pastorally short-sighted, and see everything with blurred outlines, while others appear to be pastorally blind. The latter will sit in church while choir boys make faces and whisper to one another across the chancel, and after the service will remark, ' We have no trouble with our boys ; they always behave well.' They will speak of their mission services as reaching men ' who have never heard of the name of Christ ', and will preach to them and

[1] Cp. George Herbert, *A Priest to the Temple, or The Country Parson*, ch. xxvi : ' Country people are full of these petty injustices, being cunning to make use of another, and spare themselves ; and scholars ought to be diligent in the observation of these, and driving of their general school-rules ever to the smallest actions of life : which while they dwell in their books they shall never find ; but being seated in the country, and doing their duty faithfully, they will soon discover : especially if they carry their eyes ever open, and fix them on their charge, and not on their preferment.'

give them tea afterwards, without noticing that they already know the popular hymns by heart. Clergymen will walk in semi-clerical garb, smoking a pipe, down Bond Street or Cheapside, where no one goes out of fashionable or commercial uniform (except, it may be, on Saturday when a relaxation is allowed)—a thing not necessarily right or wrong in itself, but impossible to any one who had eyes to see how in such quarters dress has a definite significance, since 'a small measure of wisdom' would 'teach them how they should cut their coats '.[1] Others see things vividly

---

[1] Hooker, *Eccles. Pol.*, Book V, ch. lxxviii, § 13 : ' Now what habit or attire doth beseem each order to use in the course of common life both for the gravity of his place and for example's sake to other men is a matter frivolous to be disputed of. A small measure of wisdom may serve to teach them how they should cut their coats. But seeing all well-ordered polities have ever judged it meet and fit by certain distinct ornaments to sever each sort of men from other when they are in public, to the end that all may receive such compliments of civil honour as are due to their rooms and callings even where their persons are not known, it argueth a disproportioned mind in them whom so decent orders displease.'
The first Council of Mâcon held A.D. 581 was more truculent towards the clergy who wore military or secular garb, and condemned any wearers of such an 'indecent habit' to thirty days' imprisonment on bread and water : ' Ut nullus clericus sagum aut vestimenta aut calceamenta saecularia, nisi quod religionem deceat, induere praesumat. Quod si post hanc definitionem clericus aut cum indecenti veste, aut cum armis inventus fuerit, a seniore ita coerceatur, ut, triginta dierum inclusione detentus, aqua tantum et modico pane diebus singulis sustentetur.' Quoted in Bingham's *Antiquities*, Book XVII, ch. v, § 23.

but invariably see them distorted; they are afflicted with what (justly or unjustly) is known among historians as ' Froude's disease ', or chronic inaccuracy,[1] which naturally entails confusion of judgement. Others see things clearly and accurately enough, but from lack of attention and interest get no lasting impressions that they can use afterwards. Even the most careful observer will fail to see many things just because he is familiar with them, as the beauty of the landscape is often not marked by persons who live amongst mountains and love them. Men will serve a parish for years, even preach on the need of reverence in prayer and on the influence of posture in worship, and never observe that it is impossible for any but an undersized woman to kneel between the seats as arranged in the church in which he ministers. When we come back from a journey familiar sights look quite different for a few hours, and we notice things which we never see again till the return from another journey lifts the veil once more for half a day. When looked at upside down the colours of a view start up into an unwonted vividness; but the student needs to retain this power of seeing things frankly and brightly without having to leave his work or to have a topsy-turvy outlook on life.

[1] Cp. Ch. V. Langlois et Ch. Seignobos, *Introduction aux Études historiques* (Hachette, Paris, 2nd ed., 1899), Book II, ch. v, p. 102 : Eng. tr. by G. G. Berry (Duckworth, 1898), p. 125.

Secondly, he needs completeness of vision. Just as some people whose eyes have their lenses accurately adjusted have only a small area of the retina sensitive, so many students are unable to see more than one thing at a time. Yet this is indispensable in the earlier stages of scientific inquiry. The observer cannot tell at first what is important and what is unimportant, so he must learn to see all. He must not yet draw conclusions, and therefore must not allow himself to ignore anything because it seems to be without significance. A schoolmaster has to learn to see his whole class and to be ready for any sign of anything; he must not merely look for evidences of attention to what he is saying, he must acquire 'the teacher's eye', and in the same way the student must train the pastoral eye, so as to be ready to detect any sign of any spiritual movement.

He must not rest content with what he happens to see. A man carrying a ladder only sees the part in front, but if in swinging it one way or another he forgets the part behind, disaster will be the result. So in observing results of evangelical methods a sharp look-out must be kept for possible effects of reaction in the individual, or of alienation on the part of those whom they fail to impress. Before making use of unsatisfactory workers 'because they are such good people', or giving persons of doubtful character 'another chance', or adopting anything wrong in principle (e.g. a slate club, or a vulgar hymn tune) ' because people like it and at any rate it does some good ', the inevitable effect of such action on the whole community must be foreseen. This refusal to rest content with mere personal chance experience is partly a matter of mental outlook, and partly of physical activity. Travel and change of point of view often help towards seeing the whole of a matter.

For particular interests are apt to give an unnatural sharpness for certain things and a corresponding dullness for others. A man who has made a special study, say, of the early history of Baptism will find that the words ' baptism ', ' immersion ', ' font ', catch his eye whenever they appear in a book and distract his attention from everything else. An intense interest in a popular movement will almost destroy the power of reading anything in a paper that does not relate to it, as many persons experienced at the time of the Education controversy of 1906 and the following years. Any one who is distressed at the waste of boy life involved in the continued permission of street-selling [1] will hear the cry of the children above all the noise of the traffic. However useful and necessary this acquired sensitiveness may be later to the specialist, it must be carefully guarded against in the preliminary stages of study.

---

[1] The London County Council has at last (1911) forbidden all street-selling to children of school age.

Accuracy and completeness of observation are Sharp-
necessary for any scientific work, but for good ness of
work more is required. No great advance can be tion.
made without sharpness of vision and imagination
to discover concealed facts. Nothing is too small
to be noticed, as little things often have great
effects and big things are often discovered by
slight symptoms. Flies in the ointment,[1] Cleopatra's nose,[2] Bruce's spider, and the whole science of
bacteriology, witness how continuously this fact
has been recognized in all ages.

II

Nothing is too small to be noticed, since little Signs of
things often have considerable consequences, things.
especially by accumulation. Let us take as
an illustration of this statement a list of little
things noticed on one definite occasion, selected
for no special reason, in half an hour at a church
standing well above the average for the carefulness
and reverence with which public worship is ordered.

1. The chairs were too close together, so that
a man could only kneel with discomfort, though
there was plenty of space in the church.

2. They were fastened together so that one
person moving disturbed a whole row of others.

[1] Eccles. x. 1.
[2] Cp. Pascal, *Pensées*, ed. Brunschvicg, No. 162 : ' Le nez de
Cléopâtre : s'il eût été plus court, toute la face de la terre
aurait changé.' (Cleopatra's nose : had it been shorter, the
whole face of the world would have been changed.)

3. The choir all knelt down on taking their places in the chancel : the congregation stood as they came in, then knelt, then sat, then stood up, though the choir had already said the preparatory prayer in the vestry, and each member of the congregation had done so privately when first entering the church. Moreover, the Office begins with a preparation, so there were three prayers before the service proper began.

4. The 'amens' and responses, especially the final answer before the collect of the day, were drawled out by the choir, so that the words lost all meaning, and it was impossible for the congregation to join in. To sing the last versicle and response more slowly is liturgically and musically incorrect, as it forms no close but leads directly to the following prayer, and to do so has the effect of breaking the attention of the worshippers.

5. The responses themselves were cut short by the officiating clergyman's reading the versicles too ' thick one upon another '—a fault of at least two hundred years' standing ;[1] and the first verse

---

[1] Cp. *A Companion for the Candidates of Holy Orders*, Part II, by George Bull, D.D. (1714). In *The Clergyman's Instructor*, p. 294 : ' The prayers of the Church ought to be read distinctly and leisurely ; not to be galloped over as the manner of some is, who read the prayers so fast, that they outrun the attention and devotion of the people, not giving them time to join with them, or to make their responses in their due places. . . . There are some that read the Commandments so thick one upon another, that the people have not

of the hymn was anticipated in the style usually associated with street-corner singing.

6. The front and middle gas standards in the nave only were lighted, so that the congregation had to hold their hymn-books inclined forward, with their heads bowed down in a way that prevented their singing, or else to stand sideways. Obviously the middle and back standards should have been used so that the light might have come from behind.

7. The singing was pitched too high, so that, apart from the difficulty the congregation found in joining in it, there was an ugly break between it and the 'natural voice', which was used for certain parts and degenerated into a mumble. The speaking voice should have been more musical and the singing more natural. This fault is as old as the fourth century.[1]

8. The clergyman said 'knōwledge',[2] a pronunciation perfectly admissible and correct, but 'heard time to add that excellent prayer to each of them, " Lord, have mercy upon us, and incline our hearts to keep this law." '

[1] Cp. Aug. *Conf*. x. 33, 50 : 'Tutiusque mihi videtur quod de Alexandrino episcopo Athanasio saepe mihi dictum commemini, qui tam modico flexu vocis faciebat sonare lectorem psalmi, ut pronuncianti vicinior esset quam canenti.' (It seems to me safer to do as I have heard that Athanasius bishop of Alexandria did, who made the reader of the psalm sing with such slight modulations of his voice that it sounded more like speaking than singing.)

[2] Cp. Bernard Shaw, *Pleasant Plays : Candida*, Act I, p. 87. Miss Proserpine Garnett to the Rev. Alexander Mill : ' Why do you say "knoaledge" in church though you always say " knolledge " in private conversation ? '

chiefly from clergymen ' and generally regarded as
' affected ' by laymen.

9. When the service was over the congregation
were hurried out of the church by the verger
making haste to lock the doors.

Many other similar points might, no doubt, have
been observed had any one gone with the express
intention of looking out for them, but the above
forced themselves on the attention of one of the
worshippers.

Trivial points are just the things that are not
noticed by those in authority, though they are
remarked and commented on by strangers. They
act as deterrents with special force to the latter,
especially if they are, perhaps, making their first
steps towards the Church. Their cumulative effect
is great and all the more serious because each is
so trifling that no one thinks of calling attention
to it, though the harm of such trifles is recognized in
schools by the teaching profession. All those men-
tioned above might easily have been corrected at
once, but till there are persons charged with duties
corresponding to those of H.M. Inspectors of Schools
in the educational world the clergy must rely on
their own spiritual and personal alertness of vision.

Small signs of important things.
Important matters are often discovered by
slight clues. When the student has learned to
notice little things he will constantly be finding
that they are symptoms of big things. In time
he will learn ' to see the world in a grain of sand,'

and to learn something of 'what God and Man is' from a flower.

Thus, for example, he may sit next to some one at a service in St. Paul's Cathedral and notice that he cannot find his places in a Prayer Book and does not kneel down for the prayers. Looking round he sees the numbers that are similarly listless and bewildered. He realizes that the mass of Englishmen are ignorant of the simplest customs of the Church of the country; the reason clearly is that they have never been taught them. This opens up the whole question of education; first, the whole political question in all its complexity; then that which would still remain under the fairest laws, the whole problem of the nature of religious training and the best methods of carrying it out.

Or, to take another example, he is present at a choir practice. The question whether it is desirable to practise in the chancel of the church, or to 'sing over the chant to the Gloria' may rise in his mind, and he may be tempted to dismiss it as of little importance. Yet behind it lie really serious matters of which it is but a part. The whole problem of the 'ex-choir boy' and of his too frequent moral and religious downfall; behind that the question of payment and of the frank commercialism that he may possibly find behind the whole system of boy choirs; behind that the question of its effect on the whole attitude towards the Church of the working classes from which the boys are drawn. Or, following up a train of thought in a different direction, he may consider the effect on the spiritual life of the congregation of entrusting the interpretation of the main portions of the liturgy to a band of uneducated boys ; which leads on to the whole question of the right place of music in public worship, and on again to the rival policies of trying to draw men to Christ by popular attractions, or by the Cross.

Or, again, he may be in a church where the whole adult portion of the choir communicates at a sung service on the first Sunday in the month. He may notice that they are the only men of a particular class and type who do so. It cannot be mere chance, nor can it be imagined that all the practising Christians of that class happen to be musical. Here is a symptom of something gravely wrong ; which raises in another way the questions of the place of music in public worship, whether tests should be imposed or members admitted to choirs by proper references, and of the unreality of having words sung by people who do not believe them.[1] Such trains of thought may be started by observation of some very small detail, and may reveal how enormous is the unexplored field which

---

[1] It is not uncommon to choose the hymn containing the lines:

We come, obedient to Thy Word,
To feast on heavenly Food,

to be sung in order that the congregation may have time to leave the church while they are singing it.

exists hidden, for the most part, from the eyes of those who should be working in it.

III

These bigger problems have to be attacked. It is useless merely to deal with symptoms. But first the power to see things both big and little must be acquired. Till this has been gained there can be no certainty in ordinary pastoral work, nor can there be any real grappling with larger issues. To see little points as they are is the first step towards getting free from wasting time over trivialities while leaving serious matters to go by default.[1]

Such power of sight brings little satisfaction to its owner, and perhaps it is fortunate that there are natural limits to our view. For to see opportunities and not to be able to use them, to have clear eyes for danger coming and not to be able to ward it off, tends to throw the minds of men, like that of Cassandra, off their balance, unless they also have the power of refusing to see the distant scene as they step out, or are granted that which she was denied, the right to take arms against a sea of troubles, to oppose them, and so to bring them at least a little nearer to their end.

[1] This lack of wide observation invalidates much even of our best work such as that undertaken by Mr. Charles Booth in his *Religious Influences of London*. The excellently marshalled array of facts is largely composed of the opinions of men who, though in the thick of the work, have never learned to see with sufficient accuracy or width.

CHAPTER II

THE WORK OF CRITICISM

THE mere accumulation of facts is useless unless they are sifted in some way. They tend to become overwhelming in their mass, and some principle of selection is called for. It is necessary to know which are well attested and trustworthy, and which of those that stand the test are important. It is imperative both to see and to understand : criticism is therefore needed ; first, criticism of accuracy, then criticism of value.

I

Criticism of accuracy. Criticism of accuracy must first be applied to observation. This is not superfluous even for those who are naturally able to see exactly. We are all liable to hallucinations in which a number of accidental resemblances, seen accurately enough, prevent our noticing points of difference. Mistakes between things similar are no less frequent. A clear but superficial observance of customs easily classes as 'almost Roman Catholic' forms of worship entirely uninspired by any Latin spirit. Our powers of vision vary with changes of health and mood, at different times of the day, according as we are tired, put out, hopeful or anxious, fasting or full.[1]

Moreover, in all the higher studies we are met with this peculiar difficulty—that for scientific observation impartiality is required ; but to be indifferent, if it were possible to be so in the matter with which Pastoral Theology deals, is precisely the way to see nothing. A purple robe may be only ' sheep's wool dyed with juices of a shell-fish ' ; and you may be ' disenchanted of the delights of song and dance and the pancratium, if once you decompose the melody into its constituent notes and ask yourself one by one " Is this the spell I own ? " ' [2] but by such a process a yellow primrose will never be even a yellow primrose, and to ' apply the process to life as a whole ' is to make yourself deaf to all its harmonies. We inevitably ' receive but what we give ', and just the caring for a thing that makes us sharp to detect all that touches it nearly, makes us see what we want to see and decide on grounds already chosen.

We unconsciously make selection of the examples that come before us. We describe exceptions as typical of the Germans, of the middle classes, of Nonconformists, and fail to take account

Unconscious selection.

[1] Cp. Keble, *The Christian Year*, the Twenty-fourth Sunday after Trinity :

Our eyes see all around in gloom or glow—
Hues of their own, fresh borrowed from the heart.

[2] Cp. Marcus Aurelius Antoninus to Himself, Book VI. 13 and Book XI. 2, tr. G. H. Rendall (Macmillan, 1898).

of the mass of the normal; a closer criticism reveals to us that by 'typical' we mean something peculiar in the group that could not have been found elsewhere, but is no further characteristic of the whole. In comparing classes of men we, without realizing what we are doing, pit the best of one against the worst of another, the ideal of our own side with the actual of the alien. We are biased by prejudices of country, of church, or of social status, or even by reaction from any of these prejudices which some time before had swayed us. We alter our standards of judgement even as we compare men, if one belongs to those of whom more is expected. We judge David with severity and are inclined to regard Tiglath Pileser as an enlightened monarch; Constantine is condemned and Julian praised. We can at times even feel the change as it is made in ourselves; we see a man casually and set him down as the natural healthy-minded 'man in the street, from whom the clergy could learn so much'; we look at his collar and see he is a parson and, by a sudden revulsion of feeling, we judge him with unreasonable strictness. In forming opinions of working men, of commercial society, of people who go to church, of the poor, of doctors, of shop-assistants, of charitable workers, unless we are rigorously critical and set ourselves to notice a definite number of individuals impartially, we shall inevitably select the best dressed, the most striking, the eccentric, those who please us or those who irritate us, and, ignoring the others, shall attribute their qualities to the whole. Even an anxiety to be fair will make us, by an inverted prejudice, applaud what is bad and run down the praiseworthy.[1]

These tendencies are a continual source of error, and call for careful self-criticism in the student ; but they are further complicated when the matters dealt with are the opinions of others which form so large a part of the data of Pastoral Theology. Here we are met at once by the natural difficulties of language in which the opinions must be expressed. Hardly any word has exactly the same meaning for any two men. By an undenominational use of the Apostles' Creed you may get a striking appearance of unity, but that is only because each of the various bodies of men that have split up over their interpretation of it attaches an entirely different meaning to its phrases.

Criticism of terms.

[1] Pascal, *Pensées*, ed. Brunschvicg, No. 615 : ' On a beau dire. Il faut avouer que la religion chrétienne a quelque chose d'étonnant. " C'est parce que vous y êtes né," dira-t-on. Tant s'en faut ; je me roidis contre, pour cette raison-là même, de peur que cette prévention ne me suborne ; mais, quoique j'y sois né, je ne laisse pas de le trouver ainsi.' (Whatever may be said, it must be admitted that the Christian religion has something astonishing in it. Some will say, ' This is because you were born in it.' Far from it ; I stiffen myself against it for this very reason, for fear this prejudice bias me. But although I am born in it, I cannot help finding it so.)

Words vary, too, for the same man as through the stages of his life they gather to themselves new associations—a matter which affects our whole judgement of prayers and hymns. These variations between men are increased with increasing differentiations of class, of age, or of race. Uneducated people will decry dogmas and clamour for religious bodies to state their tenets with authority ; they will object to the Church Catechism and ask for their children to be taught the Creed, the Lord's Prayer, and the Ten Commandments with simple explanations instead. This difference in the use of words touches parish work continually ; sons of professional men would never stand being called ' lads ', while sons of artisans will join ' lads' classes ' without seeming to mind it. A choirmaster will be voted friendly by men of one particular social grade if he addresses them as ' boys ', while the same term applied to undergraduates at the University, or to working men in the south of England, would be regarded as an impertinence. So in mission work we are apt to forget that the language of acts has even a greater variation than that of words. We do not know what to be baptized or to communicate means to men of blood or traditions entirely different from ours, and we have to act in extraordinary ignorance of what lies beneath the surface of their lives.

Moreover, the mass of people are not accustomed

to the exact use of words even in the senses in The ex-
act use
of words. which they themselves use them ; they resent any attempt to insist on it, and call it ' quibbling '. But obviously before we can plan out special methods for ' the poor ' with any hope of success, we must be clear in which of its many senses the word is used.[1] Organization is decried by people who really by the term mean disorganiza-tion, but their dislike of the word bars the way to the thing. A ' service ' may be a cinematograph show, a concert, or even a gramophone repetition of the sounds of an office actually sung in church, but the ambiguity of the word will prevent many from recognizing that the conception of worship has, as a matter of fact, utterly passed out of their lives.[2] How this inexactitude of terms is played upon by politicians may be realized by a study of the use of such expressions as 'sectarian', 'full

---

[1] Cp. *Principles of Parish Work*, ch. vi.

[2] Cp. the *Westminster Gazette*, September 1910 : ' Cinemato-graph pictures in the Grace Methodist Episcopal Church of New York on Sundays is the latest device to attract wor-shippers. . . . Dr. R——, Pastor of the Church, says there is accommodation for 1,600 persons, and every seat was occupied on Sunday night to witness views of the Passion Play at Ober-ammergau, interspersed with pictures illustrating reindeer hunting and logging in the Northern Countries. *The service* [sic] *was so animated and so successful that it has been decided to give week-night exhibitions also.* Admission is free on Sunday nights, and, while moving pictures of the proper sort will, it is hoped, always be a feature of Grace Church, there will also be hymns and a short missionary address.'

popular control', 'simple Bible teaching', or 'the will of the people '.[1]

Again, some persons attach an exact but false meaning to words. With such the accurate thinker has no common ground. The phrases used by Christian Scientists appear to have some definite meaning to their users, but to most educated men they are mere jargon. No one can listen to the ordinary street-preacher without realizing that he is obviously speaking of some real spiritual experience, though the words with which he tries to explain it, or to call it forth in others, may be grotesquely meaningless if taken in their natural sense, and offer an easy target for the gibes of the freethinker.

The con-
nexion
The mass of men have little sense of the connexion of words and meaning, especially in

[1] Cp. Hooker, *Eccles. Pol.*, Book III, ch. iii. 1 ; ' The mixture of those things by speech which by nature are divided, is the mother of all error. To take away, therefore, that error which confusion breedeth, distinction is requisite. Rightly to distinguish is by conceit of mind to sever things different in nature, and to discern wherein they differ. So that if we imagine a difference where there is none, because we distinguish where we should not, it may not be denied that we misdistinguish. The only trial whether we do so, yea or no, dependeth upon comparison between our conceit and the nature of things conceived.'

In the political world ' the people ' means the majority of male voters, in parochial work ' your people ' generally means the wives of artisans and labourers. An examination of the various meanings assigned to the words 'natural' or 'marriage' will reveal the practical seriousness of such equivocations.

controversy. It would be terrible if it were not so.
They will make gross and unfounded charges of
dishonesty and immorality against their opponents,
which shock us till we realize that they are used
in a purely Pickwickian sense. Others, again,
have no sense of the need of binding words to
action. When you have at last got them to see
a point they say, 'I agree with you in theory,
but in practice I should do just the opposite.'
They are like the man who said, 'I go, sir,' and
went not, and are proud of their fault. When
wishing to mock the scholar, who thought that he
was consulting Dr. Faust and desired advice on the
study of Theology, Mephistopheles counselled him
when ideas failed to fall back on words to fill the
gap.[1] Till the necessity for criticism of terms is
realized in Pastoral Theology we shall be merely
ploughing the sands.

[1] Goethe, *Faust* :

> Denn eben wo Begriffe fehlen,
> Da stellt ein Wort zur rechten Zeit sich ein.
> Mit Worten lässt sich trefflich streiten,
> Mit Worten ein System bereiten,
> An Worte lässt sich trefflich glauben,
> Von einem Wort lässt sich kein Iota rauben.

> (For just where all ideas fail us,
> Comes an apt word to fill the vacancy.
> With words you can argue, and subtly twist 'em,
> From words construct a goodly system ;
> In words believe, nor can you whittle
> From a word a single jot or tittle.)

Tr. A. G. Latham, Dent's 'Everyman's Library'.

Criti-
cism of
penetra-
tion.

Again, criticism of penetration is needed. We may easily fall into error from asking leading questions. There are men who on the slightest encouragement will declare every cloud in the sky to be like a whale. Sometimes answers are given out of politeness : people say what they think you want them to say ; they do not want to hurt your feelings. Men met casually in the train will begin to discuss Church news as if they were churchgoing Christians ; after a quarter of an hour's conversation they will often talk with a frankness that reveals their entire lack of fixed moral or religious belief, and their utter need of a guiding faith. At other times answers will be given merely from rudeness, and on these will be built up a theory of the existence of a ' prejudice ' that is broken down by shaking hands. Others will give answers out of bravado from a desire to show their independence, or from an inverted Pharisaism whose professors thank God that they are not as other men are, that they never go to church, fast, or give tithes. Sometimes answers are given merely for the pleasure of grumbling. Before evidence of any value can be extracted from such material, criticism must be called into play to penetrate to what lies behind.[1]

---

[1] Pascal, *Pensées*, ed. Brunschvicg, No. 105 : ' Qu'il est difficile de proposer une chose au jugement d'un autre, sans corrompre son jugement par la manière de la lui proposer ! Si on dit : '' Je le trouve beau ; je le trouve obscur,'' ou autre

II

Once more, criticism of worth is needed. Things Criti-
accurately seen and truthfully described may, cism of
after all, be of very little importance.   The worth.
capacity to witness and judge possessed by the
person who gives evidence of them must be estimated.   Sometimes this may in a single sentence
be shown to be so small that the rest may be

chose semblable, on entraîne l'imagination à ce jugement, ou
on l'irrite au contraire.   Il vaut mieux ne rien dire ; et alors
il juge selon ce qu'il est, c'est-à-dire selon ce qu'il est alors,
et selon que les autres circonstances dont on n'est pas auteur
y auront mis.   Mais au moins on n'y aura rien mis : si ce
n'est que ce silence n'y fasse aussi son effet, selon le tour et
l'interprétation qu'il sera en humeur de lui donner, ou selon
qu'il conjecturera des mouvements et air du visage, ou du
ton de la voix, selon qu'il sera physionomiste : tant il est
difficile de ne point démonter un jugement de son assiette
naturelle, ou plutôt, tant il en a peu de ferme et stable.'
(How difficult it is to submit anything to the judgement of
another, without prejudicing his judgement by the manner
in which we submit it !   If we say; 'I think it is beautiful,'
'I think it obscure,' or the like, we either entice the imagination into that view, or irritate it to the contrary.   It is better
to say nothing ; and then the other judges according to what
really is, that is to say, according as it then is, and according as
the other circumstances, not of our making, have contributed to
it.   But at least we shall have added nothing, unless it be that
silence also produces an effect, according to the turn and interpretation which the other will be disposed to give it, or as he
will guess from gestures or countenance, or from the tone
of the voice, if he is a physiognomist.   So difficult is it not
to upset a judgement from its natural place, or rather so
rarely is it firm and stable !)

ignored.[1] The variations in judgement due to sex must be reckoned with ; some areas of Church life are coloured with ultra femininism of opinion, in others there may be no woman's knowledge to correct the limitations of a purely masculine outlook. Sincere but false explanations of events may be given, as when a conversion for which forces were long ago preparing is attributed to the giving of a tract, or when the existence of physical causes leading to a period of temperance is not realized and a pledge is given the credit for the change. There is no reason in most cases to doubt the sincerity of the mission reports and advertisements that describe religious work, but, unless they are read critically, conclusions based upon them will be sometimes found to be very misleading.

[1] For instance, if we read in a book that ' it is perhaps, on the whole, not advisable to make a practice of giving to children who are sent by their parents to ask for relief ', we need not trouble to read further. A writer who speaks in such hesitating terms about a plain and serious evil cannot have sufficient knowledge of the social world around him to give any valuable advice on other similar but less obvious matters. Some persons, on the other hand, are capable of forming sane and balanced judgements on most things, but are obsessed by particular prejudices. So long as they can ' keep King Charles's head out of the Memorial ' their evidence can be relied on. Thus there are men who, though reasonable in other respects, are quite ready to believe that every monastery has secret underground passages or to swallow the stories of ' escaped nuns ', just as for many years it was believed that Christians ate human flesh, and even to this day Jews are accused of sacrificing Christian children.

Criticism of the worth of facts as evidence is no less necessary. Identical results may be due to widely different causes. A decline of convictions for drunkenness all over London on a particular Good Friday may have accompanied a change in the weather as well as the institution of special services in music-halls, but more evidence is needed before the result can be safely attributed to one or the other cause. The same phenomena in a town or country congregation may have the same significance, but it is uncritical to assume that this is the case where the circumstances are so different.[1]

Criticism may be helped by the test of analogy. The test of ana-logy. We may gauge the intrinsic probability of a statement by comparing it with what we know to be true in other cases. When an artisan gives it as his opinion that, if a man is ' persecuted for going to church ' by his mates, it is probably his own fault for making himself disagreeable, and that working men respect a man who has a religion and sticks to it, we at once believe him because his experience is exactly paralleled in the society we know by direct knowledge : a single piece of such evidence is more convincing than a dozen

[1] Cp. Hooker, *Eccles. Pol.*, Book I, ch. viii. 3 : ' A common received error is never utterly overthrown, till such time as we go from signs to causes, and show some manifest root or fountain thereof common unto all, whereby it may clearly appear how it hath come to pass that so many have been overseen.'

stories of 'persecution' coming only from the 'persecuted'. When an Indian Christian declares at a congress that there is no very obvious difference between the lives of those of his countrymen who are churchgoing Christians and the pious heathen around them we are at once convinced that he is telling the truth, because the case is precisely the same in our experience at home. When another says that though the difference is scarcely perceptible yet there is *all* the difference—the same difference as there is between a man going forwards and one going backwards—we at once believe him too for the same reason.[1]

The test of personal experience.

Finally, the test of personal experience may be applied. If in doubt whether an invitation to tea 'to get hold of' some one is likely to have any spiritual result, a recollection of similar experiments practised on us in former days will be of considerable value as a touchstone with which to test the soundness of our contemplated plan. All these various methods of criticism must be employed on any point to which they may be relevant before we can use it with confidence as evidence.

[1] Cp. The Cambridge Church Congress, Oct. 1910.

III

At present the mass of our experimental and practical Church Work is based on untested assumptions. Little stories of the sayings and doings of uneducated people unaccustomed to think clearly or act consistently, heard and noted quite by chance and repeated quite uncritically, are considered sufficient evidence on which to base undertakings that demand a vast expenditure of time and money. Mere tradition is held enough to justify the continuance of useless works which are exhausting the lives and courage of devoted men. The very idea of questioning their value is regarded as a sign of slackness, so absent is the critical sense. Yet criticism is the second essential for thorough work. We must first clear away the mass of inutilities that cumber the ground, and give the worker some leisure to think and an open field to work in. 'For when a person assumes a first principle which he does not yet know, on which unknown first principle depends a web of intermediate propositions and the final conclusion, by what possibility can such mere admissions ever constitute science?'[1] On the other hand, the area from which our information is drawn increases

The present need of criticism.

---

[1] Plato, *Republic*, Book VII. 533 c : ᾧ γὰρ ἀρχὴ μὲν ὃ μὴ οἶδε, τελευτὴ δὲ καὶ τὰ μεταξὺ ἐξ οὗ μὴ οἶδε συμπέπλεκται, τίς μηχανὴ τὴν τοιαύτην ὁμολογίαν ποτὲ ἐπιστήμην γενέσθαι;
οὐδεμία, ἦ δ' ὅς.

enormously directly we adopt critical methods. We learn from every one and everything. The world becomes our parish. Just as to the critical reader the whole realm of literature becomes a source of knowledge because even bad books set him thinking whether he could do better, and false assertions compel him to seek the truth, so, too, the critical spirit that is wanted in Pastoral Theology is not ' der Geist, der stets verneint ', but that which aims not at destruction but fulfilment.

Caution and humility.

The critical attitude will give, too, the right spirit for Pastoral Work. It will make us cautious and humble. It is the uncritical who, expecting too much, are disappointed, who live in the shows of the world, who fail in charity when the facts of life force on them the knowledge that man is fallen. It is the critic who does not become cynical, who can be patient because, in some things at least, he has got to the bed-rock of truth. He can bear to find out that many of those who are held in high reputation are unworthy of the place they hold in the minds of men, without losing faith in human nature, because the same severe methods have discovered the goodness and worth of those, the larger number, who are rejected of men. For, it cannot be too often repeated, the best criticism is that which detects the good in everything. Any one can find fault ; it often takes a critic to discover matter for praise. The old legend said that the Saviour alone could find beauty in the carcass of a dog,[1] and to develop the faculty of appreciation should be the constant aim of the student and of the worker.[2]

[1] Cp. Hastings' *Dictionary of the Bible*, extra vol., art. ' Agrapha ', p. 351 ; *Agrapha from Mohammedan Sources*, 33 : ' Malik, son of Dinar, said, Jesus one day walked with his apostles, and they passed by the carcass of a dog. The apostles said, How foul is the smell of this dog ! But Jesus said, How white are its teeth ! '

[2] Cp. B. R. Haydon to Miss Mitford, in E. V. Lucas' *The Second Post*, p. 114 : ' Whatever you praise to Jeffrey, he directly chuckles out some error that you did not perceive. Whatever you praise to Scott, he joins heartily with yourself, and directs your attention to some additional beauty. Scott throws a light on life by the beaming geniality of his soul, and so dazzles you that you have no time or perception for anything but its beauties : while Jeffrey seems to revel in holding up his hand before the light in order that he may spy out its deformities.'

CHAPTER III

SELECTION AND CLASSIFICATION

Constructive work.

THE next step is to sort our facts. This becomes possible only after the ground has been cleared, and the mass of data reduced to manageable size by criticism. A negative attitude is always a necessary preliminary to positive work, whether in weeding a garden, clearing a forest, or going through the first stages of creating a science; but it is only a preliminary. We must be critically constructive; otherwise seven other devils will quickly re-occupy the swept and garnished house.

There are numberless things waiting to be done, in the parish and in the world; little things for the rank and file to undertake, and big things for leaders to be charged with. They are left undone because we do not see clearly, because men are overburdened with useless work. The next thing needed, therefore, is concentration. We need to get some order into our mass of observed and tested facts, to sort them into groups so that we may discover the laws that bind them together, and to base our efforts on a sound knowledge of their working.

I

First we must collect all the data that have been selected by criticism as valuable ; we need to see them as a whole. Then they must be sorted into groups as they bear on this or that subject. We must learn to see common elements in different things, to notice their connexion one with another, and to mark how far the common features extend. This is just what the uneducated cannot do ; their minds are not accustomed to abstract thought or to comprehensiveness of vision, and they invariably attempt to generalize from single instances, to believe that summer is made by a single swallow.

This grouping of data may be made by area— perhaps the simplest method of classification : we may study the features of religious life in a parish, in the diocese, in its national forms, or in the foreign mission-field. Or it may be by subject ; we may divide the matter as suggested above in Book III, ch. iv, and make a detailed study of some branch of Liturgiology, of Homiletics, or of ' Church Work '.[1]

When the particular leading idea has been chosen we must keep to it. We must be blind to all others for a time, simply leaving aside all

Collection and sorting of data.

Concentration on the subject in hand.

[1] The great majority of books hitherto written are handbooks for parish work or treatises on Homiletics.

data that are irrelevant, and only viewing those
that have any bearing on the subject in their
particular features that bear on our special study.
We must refuse to be drawn off the scent by red
herrings. Much of the present-day consideration
of points in Pastoral Theology is rendered futile
by the intrusion of discussions on Socialism, or
of heated arguments about 'Ritualism', which,
even if they have points of contact with the
matter in hand, are apt to lead the student off
at a tangent. Such questions should be thoroughly
discussed in their right time and place, and then
be considered done with, so that other questions
may be examined with equal thoroughness, as if
there were no politics or ceremonial in the world.
In concentration on any subject a sharp look-out
should be kept for relevant evidence where it is
least expected, and the student must learn to
disentangle it from the surroundings in which
it is found. Thus, for instance, in considering the
bearing of the English Sunday School system on
the sense of family feeling it is irrelevant for any
one to say, ' I find my Sunday Schools a great help,'
nor is it necessarily an argument in their favour to
point to former scholars who now go to church, if
their habits are really due to the example of their
fathers and the real factor is that of the influence
of the home. The student must learn to calculate
the force, the extension, and the limits of any
matter that he sets himself to find out about, and

must avoid adding to his stock of examples by logical fallacies.

The student of theory should aim at being able to refer every phenomenon to a whole, and the practical student should try to do every piece of work in conscious subordination to some larger scheme or plan. Often isolated facts will have to be left suspended in his mind till others are discovered which will join with them to form a group. He should not be in too great a hurry to classify all that he sees ; notes made will often remain merely indexed for a long time without throwing light on any larger issue. He must let his framework of classification form itself, as novelists say the plots of their stories do, and he must not be in too great a hurry to arrive at definite conclusions. *Every detail to be referred to a whole.*

Having chosen his special subject and having collected and grouped all the available data, he should aim at securing completeness of evidence. He must extend his area of observation—a thing impossible to do before, as the mass of things seen would have been merely confusing. He may study his subject in several parishes, either by travelling or by associating others with him in his quest. In adopting the latter method he will try to get inquirers of different types and temperaments. He may, for instance, set himself to study the real opinion held by working men of Mothers' Meetings, or that of the ordinary man on the current methods *Completeness of evidence by (1) extended observation ;*

of preparation for Confirmation, or the extent to which ' the eleven o'clock service ' really meets the spiritual needs of Englishmen, or the view of the Parade Service taken by the rank and file of our soldiers, or the nature of the casual applicants for help that come to the clergy. If he systematically notes all the opinions expressed by, say, fifteen men chosen at random, or of a dozen soldiers in a regiment, or investigates half a score of the stories of men who come to beg—if a larger number is attempted it will probably become known that he is conducting an inquiry and he will not get normal evidence—his work will have a certain limited value, but it will have no claim to be considered really scientific until he has got at least a dozen others to do the same, and has compared their observations with his own. Such a systematic extension of personal experience is necessary if we are to ascertain the soundness of a popular judgement, the extension and vitality of a custom, the causes of a failure, or the intensity of a social and religious problem.

(2) sustained observation. Observation may be further extended in other ways. We may supplement our present-day evidence by that gleaned from the past. Certain features are persistent in Church life. The practical difficulty of Old Testament interpretation, with the problem of its teaching, has a continuous history from the times of Marcion and of the Gnostics, through mediaeval allegorism, post-

Reformation Puritanism, the Enlightenment, and nineteenth-century free-thinking, down to the present day. It is no new thing, and this fact itself is reassuring in our consideration of the problem. Again, such direct observation as we have should be far more sustained. This lack of continued study of the features of religious life is a defect that is shared by social science, where there is far too little watching of the after-history of cases of 'cures' of distress or vice. There is a considerable fund of knowledge of the phenomena of parish, or local, missions owing to the fact that experienced missioners have devoted their lives to the work of conversion, and to conducting revivals. But there is practically no store of systematic evidence as to their lasting results. Stories of conversion rarely tell what the penitent was doing ten years afterwards, and the vague term a 'backslider' implies an after-history of the 'saved' of which nothing really is known, though there are examples enough to warrant the use of such a quasi-technical expression. There has been so far no thorough and exhaustive examination of the permanent results, for good or evil, of the Welsh Revival of 1905. We can only say of the Reports of certain Missions that the stories told of success have an after-history of failure, since, in spite of their number and striking character, the face of the world is not materially changed. Again, we need a sustained observation directed to various matters of the past : to trace, for instance, the growth of liturgies ; to watch the evolution of customs ; to map out the gradual coming to a clear conception of ethical questions, such as that of the nature of marriage, against periodic reactionary forces of natural instinct. We want it also in experiments in the present to watch the development of religious or social enterprises, such as boys' clubs, that we may form a reasoned opinion of their utility or a sure ground on which to settle details of their constitution.

II

The use of imagination.

The student must realize that this is a work of time. He must avoid short cuts to conclusions, and must learn when evidence is sufficient and when he must hold his judgement in suspense. But with the greatest diligence and patience certain gaps in the evidence will remain. To fill these he must call to his aid powers of imagination.

In doing this the utmost caution is needed. He must only have recourse to his own conjectures when all the relevant facts available have been collected. He may then turn to history to look for parallels to suggest what is probably the case to-day. A study of the Early Church will tell him what to expect in India at the present time. An examination of the part played by the fear of Hell in furthering the spread of Christianity in the days of persecution—one of Gibbon's famous five causes—will, when he has sought for signs of it in primitive literature, guide him in estimating the part, great or negligible, that it plays now in the minds of people whom he cannot directly approach. Or he may go to other countries to borrow light with which to illuminate dark corners of his own. He may study religions comparatively and find in savage customs similarities to modern usages, which may, or may not, be survivals of primitive beliefs. He may turn to Lutherans or to Roman Catholics abroad, looking for practices the meaning of which is explicit there, and guess what may be implied in analogies at home. He may study Oriental Christian rites and so come to an understanding of our own country's ritual that a mere observation of Latin races would never induce.

Or he may look for analogies rather than exact parallels. The calling of a schoolmaster will suggest much as to the special qualities needed by the clergyman, the aims and organization of his work, the furniture and fabric of his church, the psychology of his congregation, and his relations to his fellow workers. Similarly other professions may be made to contribute suggestions : that of the doctor and social worker for the study of spiritual therapeutics ; of the statesman for the problems of ecclesiastical government ; of the business man for those of advertisement, that

Analogy.

Christ may be ' openly set forth crucified '[1] before the eyes of the people ; of the merchant for those of extension and organization that the talents entrusted to the Church may be traded with till He come, or at least given to the banker to earn their natural usury. We need above all the type of mind that is quick to imagine what other people feel and think. Just as in the earlier stage these methods were to be used for criticism, so now they must be called into play in the service of constructive reasoning.

III

Giving the right to speak.

Thus with time and experience the student will have earned a right to speak. Hasty and traditional judgements that are repeated from year to year, such as those on the relative force of written and spoken sermons, conventional precepts such as those appearing in little books on the practice of public and private prayer, will be swept away. For them will be substituted a direct critical sustained examination of what as a matter of fact does tell, and why it tells, in preaching and in other matters; of how, as a matter of fact revealed by a positive method of observation, men do pray, and have prayed, in private and in common. When this has been effected opinions will be transformed into scientific knowledge.

[1] Gal. iii. 1 προεγράφη, ' Was posted up, placarded.' Lightfoot, ad loc.

It will give also a sense of proportion. To examine the extent, duration, and intensity of any movement will enable us to see it as it is. When the various parts of modern religious life have been so set in clear light, we shall have ground to go upon to see which are the big things and which are trivial and unimportant. When this has been realized effort will be concentrated on the things that matter to the lasting benefit of the Church and the World.

A sense of proportion.

CHAPTER IV

GENERALIZATION AND CONSTRUCTIVE WORK

Genera-
lization.
GENERALIZATION, the last stage of scientific work, becomes possible when we have a sufficiency of tested and ordered data—a sufficiency, that is, as regards time, area, and number. When the phenomena of any matter under observation have been examined along the line of history, with a wide view, and with scrutiny as to their frequency we can then form sound conclusions as to its duration, extent, and intensity. These conclusions resolve themselves into permanent laws independently of our presuppositions, and even though these laws are only generalized observations of our own minds they give good warrant for a belief in archetypal laws that are eternal principles working by the Divine Will and having an actual existence in the mind of God.

With these laws we can co-operate, and act with certainty as to results. Just as Nature is conquered by being obeyed, and the knowledge of the 'laws of Nature' gives man such an immense power when dealing with physical forces, so in Pastoral Theology a knowledge of its laws will give to our work a spiritual force which will always be absent as long as we 'do things ourselves'; we shall be able to co-operate with God's laws and to act with confidence where now our methods are tentative and hesitating.

We shall be helped to settle all questions of obligation when we have learned to separate what is permanent from what is temporary or local ; we shall be in a position to judge how far any practice can be demanded of all, of one sex or age, or how far it is merely a matter of personal choice or inclination. We shall be able to estimate more surely what are the chances that a scheme will work, and, instead of dissipating our force as at present, we shall be able to see how work may be made most effective. In short, we shall be able to test all by the old Catholic canon, *quod semper, quod ubique, quod ab omnibus.*

I

Some features of religious life will at once be revealed as temporary. We shall be able to trace their existence to the influence of movements of the time. Thus, when reviewed on a scale large enough, the relation of the peculiar discipline of the Roman Church to the military spirit becomes clear. Other features appear in history and come to stay. Customs based on new discoveries take a permanent place in civilization ; thus evening services, as we know them, have come into existence with the improvement of artificial light ; the deepening of private devotion, and the spread of its literature which

(1) some features temporary ;

seems to have taken its rise in the early part of the seventeenth century, are directly connected with the cheapening of printing. In other cases, maybe, our traditional judgements will be corrected; and 'good old-fashioned methods' will turn out, on careful investigation, to be merely mid-Victorian developments of comparatively recent date.[1]

(2) others continuous and developing; Other features, again, are continuous and developing rather than permanent. They last, but change by a gradual evolution. When we have realized this we can appreciate the undeveloped stages, and often it is only when we have studied the origins of institutions that we can understand their later forms. By such means we shall learn to settle the rights and wrongs of Mediaevalism, to avoid the bigotry of ultra-modernism equally with the faddiness of those who live in the past alone. We shall be ready to adapt and adopt old customs, and to guide their transformation in the right way. Thus the old spirit of pilgrimage may be found to be based on a permanent instinct, which may be working out in good or bad directions in Sunday School treats, Communicants' outings, diocesan gatherings, cross-visits of members of societies, demonstrations for or against movements in the Church or Bills in Parliament. Again, we shall be able to see when ideas are advancing or going back; whether, for instance, modern views

[1] Cp. *Circumstances or Character?* p. 58, 'The Origins of Modern Church Work.'

on marriage are progressive or retrograde, a clear judgement about which is all the more necessary because the higher views that have been reached with so much labour are often guarded by persons who are themselves naturally of a weak or reactionary character.

Other features will be found to be permanent. When we read the works of great men in the past we are conscious of no anachronism. Mankind has changed little since the days of Abraham. We can read Plato's *Dialogues* without being reminded that he had no printed books, or Augustine's *Confessions* without needing to picture the details of ancient Roman civilization. Shakespeare's plays do not grow out of date, and the fact that Dickens' characters travelled by coach neither adds to, nor takes away from, their naturalness to-day. So, too, certain religious customs, broad-based on this unchanging human nature, last unchanged. This does not mean that permanent features of religious life are necessarily right or wrong, for man is fallen even if he is made in the image of God; but, good or bad, they must be reckoned with. The widespread belief in Sacraments in savage creeds as well as in that of the Church may show that Christian rites are superstitious, or that they are designed to satisfy an abiding need of man. So in all undertakings, such, for example, as that of Prayer Book revision, if permanent unchanging laws are ignored, disaster will be the result.

(3) others permanent and unchanging.

Quod semper.

Once more, much of the history of the world is repeated in the life of each individual. There are distinct parallels to the evolution of the race in the various stages of pre- and post-natal human growth. This is of utmost importance in considering questions of education. The value of the Old Testament for teaching children religion must be estimated in this light. A study of the slow elaboration of the calendar will give a strangely accurate guide to what may be expected of men to-day in observance of holy-days; the days willingly kept by universal instinct being just those which first established themselves, while those which were slow to appear, like Ascension Day, are with difficulty kept to-day. In this, as in many other questions, the macrocosm is reflected in the microcosm.

II

(1) national features;

Certain features of religious life will be shown to be of great persistence, but only within a narrow area. Of these some are national or even merely local, while others are more widespread but limited to certain sections of the people, and are due to peculiar social conditions. Thus the ' English Sunday' is confined to the lands inhabited by peoples of British origin, and the ideas which underlie it are unintelligible to men of other blood. These facts do not necessarily condemn it. It has secured for the masses the Saturday half-holiday;

it has been of immense value in eliminating
vulgarity and noisiness from at least one day in
the week ; moreover, it is what English people
like by way of a sabbath ; but as soon as its non-
catholic nature is realized, we see that its observance is not to be identified with religion. So, too,
the differences of Teutonic and Latin races, when
they are studied, reveal the limited catholicity of
customs and ways of thinking that are natural only
to the latter. The characteristics of the Celt, of
the Anglo-Saxon, of the German, Romance, and
Slavonic races have to be observed before we can
decide the legitimate differences in, as well as the
common ground of, their religious life.[1]

In studying customs of a still more restricted (2) local
extent, we have to distinguish what is due to and class
chance from what is mere local tradition, growing features;
up because it suits certain peculiar circumstances.
Again, in considering variations due to local conditions, we have to study the limits of differences
between class and class. Before trying to establish
special undertakings for the working classes, we
need to study the real nature of their religious ideas,
a matter on which we are most extraordinarily in
the dark ; we want to realize wherein their ideas are
of their class alone, and wherein they themselves
are 'most remarkable like you'. So, too, we need to
study how far new social customs, such as that of

[1] Cp. *L'Avenir de l'Église Russe*, J. Wilbois (Bloud et Cie,
Paris, 1907).

'week-ending', really affect the essence of religion; how far industrial changes render certain practices impossible—such as, for instance, the popular observance of Saints' Days—and necessitate their transformation, in this particular case, by the putting off of the festival to the following Sunday, which the same industrial changes have more widely secured as a day of rest.

(3) features universal but varying.

Other features, again, are widespread, or even universal, but vary in their form from place to place. The custom of offering candles seems to be one of these. In the East the action is apparently confined to the simple offering. In churches under Roman influence, it is united with prayer and made quasi-sacramental. In England the custom has been rooted out of religious observance except in connexion with liturgical services, though it survives in secular, birthday, and Christmas customs; the instinct, however, can be seen working in a different form in the offering of flowers in church, chiefly at harvest and other festivals and 'flower services', and in spontaneous natural practices in connexion with the graves of the dead. Other

Quod ubique.

customs are found without change everywhere; they are simply human. We want by comparison to note these universal elements of religion, to check our customs by those of others, to free ourselves from insularity. To realize that men are the same everywhere will often put us right; the idea that city churches need only be opened 'during the dinner hour ' could be corrected by looking to foreign lands where churches have always been kept open ; there it is found that they are mainly used in the morning and the evening, before and after work.   In other cases it will put us on our guard ; thus, though it would be unfair to say that at the present day undenominational-ism in England is unchristian, a study of the education question in foreign countries shows that the spirit at work at home is precisely the same that has proved itself hostile to religion generally, and militantly secularist in France.[1]

When we have recognized these facts, the prob-lem is to decide how far it is right to acquiesce in national or class differences ; how far we should keep old customs, and how far aim at uni-formity ; how far we should have ' special methods for the poor ', and how far to have them is to stereotype divisions.[2]   These are matters of utmost importance, but many of them have never been considered, still less are they settled on grounds of thorough exhaustive scientific inquiry.

III

Certain features of religious life will, however, *Quod* be found not only through all times and in all *ab omni-* places, but revealing themselves in all men.   On *bus.*

[1] Cp. ' The Education Question—Foreign Parallels,' *Church Quarterly Review*, October 1907.

[2] Cp. *Principles of Parish Work*, ch. vi.

these are built the things that can be expected of all; they underlie the matters which are generally necessary. Among these we may place the law of the Fourth Commandment, the principle of one day in seven; the leaders of the French Revolution failed to abolish Sunday; its observance in heathen lands precedes by long years the acceptance of Christianity. Again, the laws of evangelization, based as they must be on human nature and its faculties for apprehending truth, are probably as ascertainable as are the established laws of logic and rhetoric. The difficult question of the place of self-examination and confession in religious life, which comes before us in the question of preparation for Confirmation, has behind it an instinct apparently universal, on which the Roman Church has built what is perhaps the most characteristic feature of her discipline.

Varia-
tions in
inten-
sity.

But in features which are thus universal in religion there are variations even when they occur in normal forms, and we need to be aware of these if we are to judge of the intensity of religious life in any movement, and before we can act according to any definite rule. At one time it is natural to give expression to religious feeling; at another to do so jars. Unless the reasons for this are known, evangelists are sure to urge people to expression when it is absent and to check it as undesirable the moment it appears, swaying backwards and forwards in their dealing with men.

The variations between the religious customs of men and women occur within the larger unity of common elements. Statistics of religious observance are almost valueless unless due allowance is made for variations in worth and intensity in the data from which they are compiled ; without this we are sure to see success in numbers, and an intensive policy of propaganda is certain to be ignored. The aim of influencing the masses through strong centres of religious life needs a science of Pastoral Theology to explain and commend it to men.

Moreover, a consciousness of universal laws will give a sense of proportion to the whole of pastoral work. We shall no longer rest in a contented parochialism, and shall at the same time be more content to work in a parish because it is felt to be part of a whole. It will make us realize the need of a larger propaganda, in the press, on the stage, in politics, in literature ; it will deliver the preaching in the pulpit from its ecclesiastical limitations ; it will make possible a casuistry that is based on universal principles, a worship that rises above the predilections of a sex ; it will guide us to a type of church work that will find a place for the special gifts of men and women, of rich and poor, of young and old, and will prompt and empower us to combine their deeds into one active whole.

Consequence of realizing laws.

CHAPTER V

THE MACHINERY OF PASTORAL THEOLOGY

The need of machinery. It will be quite obvious that no great advance can be made in the methods of scientific study described in the last chapters without a considerable development of machinery. For all thorough work there must be a large expenditure of labour in what is often mere drudgery, which can only be patiently borne because the larger issues at stake are realized. Much of this machinery may be constructed as we go on ; part may be borrowed from other sciences. In the present state of the study of Pastoral Theology it is hardly possible to do more than suggest general outlines. The actual forms must grow up out of the habits of workers in the parish and elsewhere, but from the beginning each student must have a definite purpose in his mind, and a clear conception of the relations of his little piece of work to the whole.

I

Notes and records. For observation, which, as we saw, is the basis of all thorough work, the habit of note-taking and recording must be insisted on. We need in every parish a careful system of diary-keeping, of minutes of meetings, of periodical reports in

Parish Magazines, of detailed records of dealing with cases of individuals, of chronicles of the various stages in the experiments that prove successful or fail. That is to say, there must be a whole-hearted acceptance of business methods. There is more than a strong presumption that what is found necessary in all other large or important undertakings is necessary in the largest and most important of all. Just as the fabric of historical knowledge is built up on a careful use of note-books,[1] so pastoral knowledge must be based on accurately recorded facts. These records must be continuous and detailed. Many matters must be entered in them which seem trivial and unimportant. You never can tell what may prove to be their value. Facts which seem to have no significance may turn out to be illuminating in a way never dreamed of at the time they were noted. These entries must be made, too, according to some more or less uniform system so as to be intelligible to others than the individuals who made them, and to allow of comparison and combination of their results.[2]

---

[1] Cp. *Introduction aux Études Historiques*, par Ch. V. Langlois et Ch. Seignobos, 2me éd. (Paris, 1899), p. 81, Eng. tr. by G. G. Berry (Duckworth), p. 103 : ' The method of slips is the only one mechanically possible for the purpose of forming, classifying, and utilizing a collection of documents of any great extent. Statisticians, financiers, and men of letters who observe, have discovered this now as well as scholars.'

[2] Cp. *Principles of Parish Work*, ch. iii.

S 2

Systematic inquiries.

These continuous parochial records may be supplemented by definite methods of inquiry, in order to make available the immense store of experience possessed by the rank and file of the clergy, which is at present unused for larger ends. *Questionnaires* on special subjects issued with authority would direct their attention to special features in their work. These might be developed on the basis of visitation and diocesan returns. At present there is often considerable resentment shown to the filling up of forms and making returns, due partly, perhaps, to the fact that the purpose of them is not seen and it is believed that they are merely used for the purpose of drawing up statistics in which no one is interested, partly, it may be, to the fact that the absence of proper records makes the work very difficult, especially to those who are not accustomed to the regular methods of business. Were it seen, however, that these questions had a definite purpose, and were to be used for larger ends, the majority would answer them gladly and well, while the fact that the questions were asked would do much to call their attention to important matters which otherwise they might have overlooked.[1]

[1] For an example of such a set of questions dealing with parochial almsgiving see the list of questions sent out by the London Diocesan Committee for information to be used by the Royal Poor Law Commission, printed in my *Circumstances or Character ?* p. 136.

A systematic keeping of records would also
serve the work of criticism. The bare fact that
a thing is put down in black and white enables
us to see it from a different point of view. We do
not want to add to our labour unnecessarily, and
therefore before writing ask ourselves, ' Is this
worth recording ? ' and we very soon come to
the conclusion that a thing not worth recording
is probably not worth doing, or at least has only
a quite secondary value. But this will be mere
individual self-criticism. Some machinery must
therefore be created for the encouraging, and for
the regulating and checking, of criticism. At present we have many irresponsible complaints, and
hear nothing of the opinions of many whose judgement would be valuable, who, moreover, would
be prepared to help in mending what they think
needs reformation. Experience in all other
departments of life has proved the necessity of
carrying on business by regular meetings of
councils and committees, in order to get lay
criticism and opinion, and at the same time to
ensure its being reasonable and responsible.[1]

Councils and Committees.

In addition to this, systematic endeavours must
be made by the professional worker to see things
from other points of view. A clergyman should
arrange periodically and regularly to sit among the
congregation in church to see things as laymen
see them. He should be at liberty from time to

Cross-visits and consultations.

[1] Cp. *Principles of Parish Work,* ch. ii.

time to get out of his circle, and travel about to find out what is done elsewhere. Cross-visits should be arranged between one parish and another; consultations and discussions on different points that may arise should be regularly and formally held. Conferences with men of other professions should be organized; with teachers to discuss the practical questions of religious education, with doctors to investigate the problems of the connexion of bodily and spiritual health, with business men to bring the finance and government of the Church into conformity with recognized procedure, with social workers to bring into clear light the intimate connexion of spiritual and political welfare. All this would help enormously in clearing the ground of false or useless methods of work which now too often hamper and burden the clergy.

Diocesan inspectors.
Certain men should specialize in this work. Some system of visitation should be organized, corresponding in its way to that of H.M. Inspectors of Schools. The work of an inspector is not to find fault, but to apply a trained and critical judgement to all that he sees, in order to approve what is excellent. By travelling about he first learns what can be done, and then acts as a link between different workers, conveying the experience of one to the other, and doing something to relieve the isolation of scattered workers. In time he becomes an expert in professional knowledge to

whom others are glad to submit their projects, sure of an intelligent and attentive hearing, and with whom they can discuss their difficulties with profit. Such inspectors, again, meeting one another at diocesan head-quarters, could establish a bureau of expert knowledge from which help on practical points could be sought. In a great number of cases their observations already made would provide an answer, but as more difficult problems arise they would be in a position to consult the whole body of the clergy in the diocese, and to learn from their experience.

When some such machinery for studying the whole general work of the Church in its normal aspects has been set going, specialization in different branches will become possible. It is held by many that the young clergyman does best to begin his work in the country, or in a small town, because there he has to learn his work as a whole and in all its parts. But just as apprenticeship in a small all-round retail business may lead on to selecting one special line in wholesale trade, so many of the clergy will naturally pass on to big towns and there specialize in particular branches of pastoral work. It should be recognized that every parish in a big town is abnormal, and that to know the methods suitable to each we need a band of men who have had experience in 'poor', 'special difficulty', suburban, city, manufacturing, 'West End', or University, parishes, both in

Specialization.

the ordinary course of serving a congregation of labourers, artisans, clerks, professional men at home and in business, or students, as well as in pioneer or mission work among these classes. The Church should aim at training specialists who in their turn could train others to help them in their work.

Similarly, special subjects need special methods of treatment. These are already in operation in certain directions. Foreign Missions are being more carefully studied than ever before. There is a body of experts on Rescue and Temperance work, and numerous societies for furthering various aims. But much remains to be done. More workers specially trained are needed to extend the area of observation from which facts bearing on the various subjects are to be put together. We need far more collected evidence on their particular callings from prison and hospital chaplains, from musical experts, from those who have made a special study of preparation for confirmation or as directors of consciences, from missioners as to the impulses that lead to conversion, of those who have peculiar gifts in dealing with boys or with girls, of those whose experience lies in the training of the clergy.

Societies. The next necessity is for such men to meet in societies that will bring them together and will stimulate their interest in their chosen subject. By so meeting, they will be saved from merely going over the same ground that others have traversed; they will make possible an accumulation of material from which they will be able to deduce certain established and ascertained results that can be used for the guidance of others.

When from a wide generalization by a number of specialists such conclusions have been reached, a definite machinery of publication is needed. There should be various organs for different departments of Pastoral Theology, corresponding to the various technical and trade publications that are read by men in secular walks of life. These will serve as a medium for further study and discussion, for the ventilating of new ideas, and for submitting conclusions to criticism by a wider specialist public. Then as they become established by the consensus of experts, the machinery of congresses may be utilized, not for the impossible task of discussing new ideas—a purpose for which they are too unwieldy—but to impress ascertained truths on the general public, and to give a stamp of authority to what for some time has been familiar knowledge to those in the thick of the work. Finally, we may look to see an increasing number of monographs in different departments of the science written by experts, and taking the place of the ' little books ' by which Pastoral Theology at present is mainly represented.

Organs for publications.

II

The ideal of work

This will help to build up an ideal of scientific work for every man who aims at helping his fellow man in his relation to God. It will make the work of Pastoral Theology to be broad-based on knowledge. When men have learned to realize the connexion of principle and action, since all they based on law. do will be based on law, they will be standing on sure ground. Their work will be done vigorously, for they will have learned to work with the great forces of the spiritual universe ; it will be to the point, for they will always have a definite aim. They will cease to demand visible consequences, to rely on personal methods, to see success in crowds, or to delight in melodramatic situations. They will be content to work without obvious results, because they will know the force of unseen laws. They will not count growth by the gaining of painful inches when they realize the world-wide forces that are flooding in in silence. They will turn to big things though their part in them may be small, for they will see by the illumination of science that they are fellow workers with God.

Co-ordination of activities.

It will make possible the co-ordination of activities. Parish work, when made scientific, will become unified. The scientific worker will be enabled to see the interaction of its various parts, will use them to support each other, to present a marshalled and ordered force against the ordered and marshalled forces of sin. He will make it his care to secure co-operation of workers, to utilize every several man in his vocation and ministry. By office routine, by councils and committees, he will bring men to work together; by organization he will give the body its needed organs, will make it an organism builded together for a habitation of God the Spirit. For he will have learned to ' see life whole '.

And our work will improve. When we have realized the power of ideas, and have learned to work with them instead of by mere physical activity, evil will be attacked with knowledge, and knowledge will be backed up by the serried ranks of organized and determined fighters. We shall have learned to deliberate on principles, to formulate and carry out a policy. The work of a clergyman will be set in its true relation to other scientific work. It will be more differentiated and more thorough, and so will meet that of others on the common ground of efficiency. The clergy will be accepted as speaking with authority on the spiritual issues of the common things of life, and their lore will again take its normal place in the world of thought. The other sciences will fall into their places, helping and enlightening Pastoral Theology, and therefore themselves helped and illuminated by Christianity.

Improvement in standard.

III

Con-
clusion.

' It was said of Socrates that he brought philosophy down from heaven to inhabit among men ;
and I shall be ambitious to have it said of me that I
have brought philosophy out of closets and libraries,
schools and colleges, to dwell in clubs and assemblies, at tea tables and coffee houses.' So wrote
Addison in the tenth number of the *Spectator*—
and it has been the ambition, aye, and the prayer
of the writer, that before the day of his decease
he may at least have wrought somewhat towards
inviting science to step forth out of the laboratory
and the mart, out of the factory and the university, to dwell in theological colleges and parish
churches, in clergy-houses and parsonages throughout the land.

It is an aim that has long been constantly before
him, one that lies very near his heart, a heart
that is often sore troubled at the present state of
England's Church and people. In it he sees what
hope he can discern for times to come. If, like
Socrates when he saw philosophy assailed with un-
deserved scorn, he too has been indignant and has
expressed himself too seriously,[1] if he has offended
with his pen, may he be pardoned and may his
excuse be that, like one little less great than
Socrates and far more holy, the great pastor and
theologian St. Augustine, he desires to assert

---

[1] Cp. *Republic,* Book VII, § 536 C.

'with emphasis and oft that he can hold no lot prosperous which leaves no time for philosophy, no life blessed but that which lives therein.'[1]

[1] *Contra Academicos*, II, ii. : ' Nam cum praesens praesenti tibi exposuissem interiores motus animi mei, vehementerque ac saepius assererem, nullam mihi videri prosperam fortunam, nisi quae otium philosophandi daret; nullam beatam vitam nisi quae in philosophia viveretur.'

INDEX

Oxford: Horace Hart, M.A., Printer to the University